SADLIER
FAITH AND
WITNESS

MORALITY

A Course on Catholic Living

Rev. Paul J. Wadell, C.P., Ph.D.

William H. Sadlier, Inc.
9 Pine Street
New York, New York 10005-1002
http://www.sadlier.com

Acknowledgments

Scripture selections are taken from the *New American Bible* Copyright © 1991, 1986, 1970 by the Confraternity of Christian Doctrine, Washington, D.C. and are used by license of the copyright owner. All rights reserved. No part of the *New American Bible* may be used or reproduced in any form, without permission in writing from the copyright owner.

Excerpts from the English Translation of the *Catechism of the Catholic Church* for use in the United States of America, Copyright © 1994, United States Catholic Conference, Inc.—Libreria Editrice Vaticana.

Excerpts from the English Translation of *Right of Penance* © 1974, International Committee on English in the Liturgy, Inc. (ICEL); excerpts from the English translation of *A Book of Prayers* © 1982, ICEL; excerpts from the English translation of *Book of Blessings* © 1988, ICEL. All rights reserved.

The English translation of the Our Father, the Apostle's Creed, and the Gloria Patri by the International Consultation on English Texts (ICET).

Excerpt from *Crossing the Threshold of Hope* by His Holiness John Paul II, Translation copyright © 1994 by Alfred A. Knopf Inc.

Excerpts from "The Death of the Hired Man" and "The Road Not Taken" from *The Road Not Taken: A Selection of Robert Frost's Poems* edited by Louis Untermeyer, Henry Holt and Company, Inc.

Excerpt from *Walden* and *Civil Disobedience* by Henry David Thoreau, Penguin Classics, Viking Penguin USA.

Excerpt from *A Man for All Seasons* by Robert Bolt, Copyright © 1960, 1962 by Robert Bolt. Reprinted by permission of Random House Inc.
Copyright © Robert Bolt 1960
Reproduced by permission of Heinemann Educational Publishers, a division of Reed Educational and Professional Publishing Limited.

Cover Illustrator: Charlene Potts
Text Illustrator: Julie Pace: 19, 36, 40, 48, 56, 68, 76, 80, 88, 98, 108, 112.

Photo Credits

Jim Saylor   Lori Berkowitz
Photo Editor   *Associate Photo Editor*

Adventure Photo and Film/ Florian Werner: 62,63; Charles Gurche: 76.
Art Resource/ Giraudon: 28, 100, 115.
Myrleen Cate: 6–7 boy, 36, 40, 41 right, 42 left, 51, 52 foreground, 120 top left.
Catholic News Service: 122 left and center; Joe Rimkus, Jr.: 11, 43; Arturo Mari: 44; Michael Edrington: 118–119.
CO2, Inc./ Coscioni: 17 jeans, tickets, gym shoes, shirt.
Corbis/ Richard Hamilton Smith: 94–95.
Crosiers/ Gene Plaisted, OSC: 26, 52 background, 91, 106.
Cameron Davidson: 54–55.
FPG: 57 bottom; Dick Luria: 17 chain; Ron Chapple: 33 top right, 60 bottom, 66, 73 bottom; Michael Scott: 33 center right; Michael Goldman: 68; Telegraph Picture Library: 86–87; Arthur Tilley: 108.
Anne Hamersky: 12.
Image Bank: 59 right, 88–89; Chris Hackett: 99; Antonio Rosario: 116; Juan Silva: 122 background.
Impact Visuals/ Jack Kurtz: 84.
International Stock/ George Ancona: 60 top; Johnny Stockshooter: 60 background.
Ken Karp: 24–25, 73 center, 97 top.
Liaison International/ Susan Greenwood: 27; Dale C. Spartas: 90–91; Figaro Magazine: 121 bottom; Guy Bensadoun: 121 center; E. Scorcelletti: 122 right.
Nonstock/ Andreas Kentsch: 33 center; Fredrick Broden: 75.
Picture Cube/ David Bitters: 57 top; Frank Siteman: 57 bottom center.

Picture Perfect: 14–15.
Photonica/ Henry Horenstein: 46–47; Kacha Hurian: 70–71; T. Shinoda: 73 top.
H. Armstrong Roberts: 8, 17, 78–79; H. Abernathy: 10; R. Kord: 16.
St. Therese Office de Lisieux: 98.
Nancy Sheehan: 89 top.
Chris Sheridan: 64, 65 top, 74, 120 bottom.
Skjold Photography: 48.
Stock Market: 92, Gabe Palmer: 17 headphones, 83 left; Peter Beck: 59 left; Vivianne Moos: 82 top, Andrew Holbrooks: 82 bottom.
Srouji: 105 bottom, 120 top right.
Superstock: 34.
Tony Stone Images: 20, 65 background, 110–111, 120 top, 178; Pat O'Hara: 6–7 background; Rosannne Olson: 9; Lori Adamski Peek: 18; Randy Wells: 22–23; Kristy McClaren: 30–31; Chuck Keeler: 33 top left; Zigy Kaluzny: 33 bottom left; John Beatty: 38–39; Stephen Johnson: 41 left; David Young Wolff: 42 right; Penny Tweedie: 49, 90; Walter Hodges: 57; William Delzell: 67; Bob Torres: 72; Bruce Ayres: 81; Jacques Jangoux: 83 right; Robert E. Dammerich: 96; Steve Weber: 97 bottom; Sylvan Grandadam: 102–103; David Madison: 104; Dennis O'Clair: 105 top.
Uniphoto: 112–113.
United Nations: 65 bottom.
Viesti Associates/ Diane Ondermerp: 80.
Visuals Unlimited/ Kirtley Perkins: 33 bottom right.
George White: 58.

General Consultant
Rev. Joseph A. Komonchak, Ph.D.

Official Theological Consultant
Most Rev. Edward K. Braxton, Ph.D., S.T.D.
Auxiliary Bishop of St. Louis

Publisher
Gerard F. Baumbach, Ed.D.

Editor in Chief
Moya Gullage

Pastoral Consultant
Rev. Msgr. John F. Barry

Scriptural Consultant
Rev. Donald Senior, C.P., Ph.D., S.T.D.

General Editors
Norman F. Josaitis, S.T.D.
Rev. Michael J. Lanning, O.F.M.

Catechetical and Liturgical Consultants
Eleanor Ann Brownell, D. Min.
Joseph F. Sweeney
Helen Hemmer, I.H.M.
Mary Frances Hession
Maureen Sullivan, O.P., Ph.D.
Don Boyd

"The Ad Hoc Committee to Oversee the Use of the Catechism,
National Conference of Catholic Bishops,
has found this catechetical text to be in conformity
with the *Catechism of the Catholic Church*."

Home Office:
9 Pine Street
New York, NY 10005-1002

ISBN: 0-8215-5654-1
123456789/987

CHAPTER 1

Getting It Right

I say to the LORD,
you are my Lord,
you are my only good.

Psalm 16:2

"I can make my own decisions. I don't need anyone to tell me what to do!" Have you ever said anything like this? When it comes to living your life and making decisions, how do you know that you will be a success, that you will get it right?

Decisions and Dreams

Life can be exciting. Sometimes it seems as if we are changing and growing not only from day to day but also from minute to minute. Our dreams for the future may change just as fast. Whether we realize it or not, we are making many decisions about our lives each day. These choices can spell the difference between success and failure in life. They include decisions about money, friends, school, sports, parents, alcohol, drugs, and sexuality, just to name a few. The list seems endless! How can we ever make sense of it all? Where can we turn for answers that will help us to dream great dreams and to choose what is best?

As people of faith we turn to Jesus and the Church to help us make sense out of life. Faith helps us to make the best choices possible. Faith is the way to get it right. Some people, however, think that the life of faith is boring and not very "cool." They think religion is just about rules and regulations that are meant to take all the fun out of life.

How wrong those people are! Perhaps they cannot see the whole picture. People of faith know differently.

One day a young man came to Jesus asking for advice about life, about his dreams and the choices he had to make. He asked Jesus, "Teacher, what good must I do to gain eternal life?" In answer to the young man's question, Jesus threw out a challenge. Was the young person strong enough and courageous enough to hear Jesus' words? Would the young person take the time to listen? Find Jesus' challenge in Matthew 19:16.

This course is all about your dreams and your decisions. It is about Jesus and the answers he gives to young people, just as he did to the young man in the gospel passage. Are you ready to hear Jesus' answers for you? Do you have the courage? Are you willing to take the time?

True Goodness and Beauty

There is nothing more beautiful than a life lived well and nothing more attractive than a good person. It is the reason people were drawn to Jesus and wanted to be with him. Being with Jesus taught them that where there is goodness, there is life.

That is why we want to be around good people, why they interest us so much. What is their secret? What good people know is that in order to be truly human, we have to be moral. When we study *morality*, we learn about the beliefs, values, virtues, rules, and principles we need to know and to practice in order to do good in our actions and to be good in our lives. Morality looks at the meaning of a good life and the character of a good person. It helps us understand what it really means to love and how we must live each day.

Can a person be moral without religion or faith? This is an important question, one we will consider in this course. In general we can say that a person can be good without religion, but our religious faith gives us a special understanding of the purpose and meaning of morality.

There are many ways to think about the moral life. One way is to see it as a search for a happiness that will last. Does everyone want to be happy? Of course. Does everyone agree on the best way to find happiness? Obviously not. Sometimes what we think will bring us happiness falls short. And sometimes what we think will make us happy actually leaves us sad and disappointed and confused. Morality gives us direction. It helps us to understand what true happiness is. More than that, it helps us find such happiness for ourselves, happiness that brings peace to our hearts and satisfaction to our desires.

Morality, especially our Catholic understanding of morality, is really a matter of learning how to be the human being that God created us to be. By God's grace we have been raised to the dignity of being sons and daughters of God. The Church teaches that we should "recognize our own dignity," the dignity of those who share in God's own life (*Catechism of the Catholic Church*, 1691).

A good person knows that life is a gift, sees its beauty, and is determined not to waste it. As we begin this exploration of the Christian moral life, we must remember three things.

- Goodness is beautiful and a great power.
- Where there is goodness, there is life and real happiness.
- There is something beautiful and good, graced and promising in each of us.

Our challenge—and the whole point of morality—is to discover how we must live if the grace and promise of our lives are not to be lost.

What promising gift do you see in yourself?

9

The Way of Happiness

Can we be truly Catholic without a sense of morality? Can we be really human?

The answer to these questions is very simple: We are made in the image and likeness of God. This means that our true happiness can be found only by choosing to fulfill God's plan for us. Telling the truth, living justly, developing our consciences, keeping our promises—we need to learn and to practice all these things and more if we are to grow as human beings created in the image and likeness of God. If we are to be truly human, we cannot view morality as simply an option. Rather, we must realize that it is an absolute requirement. It is morality that keeps us faithful to ourselves as human beings made in God's image. It is morality that makes our lives together possible.

Some people may think that morality takes away our freedom. It is true that learning how to love, learning how to be a just person, and learning to keep our promises can be difficult. Sometimes it is easier to forget about others and to put ourselves first. But eventually such behavior tricks us—it does us more harm than good—because it is truly "unnatural." It is not the way we are meant to behave.

No matter how challenging it may seem, to be moral—to respect others, to be trustworthy, to be thoughtful and kind, to be willing and able to forgive—is utterly "natural." It is such behavior that makes and keeps us human. From the very moment of creation, God has placed in us a share in his wisdom and goodness. We have a natural sense of what is good and evil. We call this the natural law.

The Church teaches that the *natural law* "is nothing other than the light of understanding placed in us by God; through it we know what we must do and what we must avoid" (*Catechism*, 1955). The natural law is present in every human being and is unchangeable. It is the foundation for building the human community and all our laws.

By denying our obligation to morality, we are in a sense living in a way that is "inhuman." If we make a habit of lying, for example, not only do we lose our friends—nobody trusts or wants to be with a liar—but we also harm ourselves because we are living in a way that deeply contradicts what God calls us to be.

Searching for Goodness

Although morality sometimes challenges us, its overall aim is not to wear us down, but to help us recognize what a good and successful life is and how we need to live in order to have it. Morality is a search for such a good life, a life capable of bringing us genuine satisfaction, deep happiness and joy, and certain and lasting fulfillment. This is something all of us need to learn if our lives are to be truly successful and happy.

Sometimes, because of sin, people can misunderstand and misinterpret the natural law. That is why the teaching authority of the Church is so important in questions of morality.

Every human being must answer the call to be moral if he or she is to grow in the image and likeness of God. The call to be moral does not come to us simply from our parents, our family, or our friends. It comes to us from God, and we hear it in our hearts. There is something deep within all of us that hungers for goodness. It is the most powerful hunger of our lives, and we cannot rest until it is satisfied. The call to be moral reminds us that to be ourselves is, in the deepest sense, to be good because goodness brings us to life. Goodness is what makes us the kind of people God created us to be.

Why is morality important for us as human beings and as people of faith? The answer is simple but vital: We cannot be human without it. The great temptation for all of us is to think that sin is to our advantage or that selfishness will bring us success. But that is never true. Wise and great people know that it is goodness that brings us joy and love that gives us life. Neither goodness nor love is easy to learn or to practice, but it is exciting to think that both are what keep us human and make us like God.

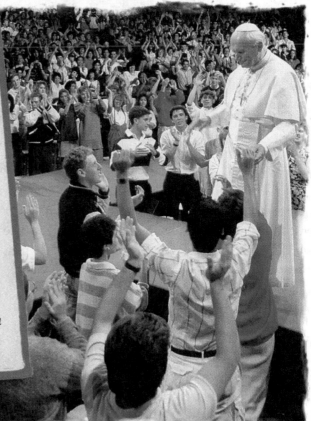

Friendship with God

When you love someone, you want to be with that person. You want that person to be happy. It is no different for God. A central message of our Catholic faith—and indeed at the heart of Christian morality—is that God is in love with us and wants what is best for us. In fact, God wants to share his own life with us.

God wants to be our friend. Not everyone thinks of God in this way, but it is true. From the very beginning of our life in our mother's womb, God is calling us to friendship. He invites us to a life of intimacy and happiness, of true closeness to him. In the Scriptures God tells us that we were created in his image (Genesis 1:26–27); we are called to be his people (Exodus 6:7); and his law has been written in our hearts (Jeremiah 31:33).

The Church has always reminded us of this wonderful truth of God's closeness to us and his offer of friendship.

How do we know that someone is truly a friend? A true friend is someone who loves us for our own sake, not for what she or he can get out of us. A true friend is someone who really wants what is best for us and who is happy when we have it. The word that best expresses a friend's feelings for us is *benevolence*, which means wishing someone well and working for what is best for him or her.

Like a good friend, God is benevolent to us. God wants what is best for us and works to see it come to pass. The greatest proof of God's benevolence is that he offers each of us a share in his own divine life. There is no better way for us to know of the friendship of God than to remember that we live because he loves us.

God gives us many signs that he wants to be our friend. God first calls us to friendship when he offers us grace. *Grace* is the gift of God's life. Grace lets us know how much God desires to share our lives, to be close to us, and to love us.

The greatest sign of God's friendship is Jesus. In the deepest sense Jesus is God's friendship "in person." Friends want to spend time with each other and to share their lives. God wants so much to share in our lives that God the Son became one of us. In Jesus Christ, God enters our world, takes on our life, and shares our history. That is why Jesus is a friend like no other.

In the deepest sense it is only possible to live a moral life because of what Jesus did for us. He transformed us through his death and resurrection. Through the power of the Holy Spirit we take part in the paschal mystery: We share in Christ's passion and die to sin; we share in his resurrection and are born to new life. Only in this way can we truly turn to God and away from sin. That is why Jesus gave us the Church to guide us in living his way. Even though after his death and resurrection Jesus returned to his Father in heaven, he still enters our world and shares our life through the sacraments, especially the Eucharist.

In what ways can you respond to God's gift of friendship?

Name some of the challenging decisions you think young people have to make today. What decisions do you think will be most important?

Have you ever thought of yourself as a living, breathing image of God? How might this idea contribute to the way you see yourself and others?

My Thoughts...

Our parish family challenges us to live a moral life in many ways. For example, parishes provide opportunities to care for the poor with clothing and food drives. Some parishes care for the homeless, the elderly, and people with AIDS. What suggestions would you have to help your parish care even more for young people who are making important decisions about life?

YOU ARE MY WITNESSES

Scripture My Life

The Bible is full of fascinating stories about God working in the lives of ordinary people. One of the most captivating is the story of the conversion of Saul (Acts 9:1–22).

Read this passage and then ask yourself whether or not you would be ready to react as Saul did.

CATHOLIC TEACHINGS

About Grace

Sanctifying grace is a participation in the very life of God that brings us into an intimate and permanent relationship with the Blessed Trinity. One of the effects of sanctifying grace is *justification*. This means that through the gift of grace we are cleansed of our sins and our hearts are turned toward God. A second effect is *sanctification*. This means that we are made holy. But we must remember that God's gift of grace demands our free response and cooperation. *Justification* and *sanctification* are important words to know because they remind us that God loves us and that we share in God's holiness.

The Key to Happiness

CHAPTER 2

May he open your heart to his law
and his commandments and grant you peace.

2 Maccabees 1:4

*Happiness is something that must be learned.
What is your reaction to this statement?
What do you believe about happiness?*

Happiness Is . . .

Believe it or not, happiness has to be learned, just as writing, reading, music, or math must be learned.

Most people do not think this way. They believe that happiness is having what they want when they want it, that it is having all their needs and desires fulfilled. They certainly would never think that sometimes happiness is hard work, even the especially hard work of changing their hearts and opening their minds that Christians call *conversion*.

Everyone wants to be happy but not all of us know where happiness is to be found. We wish for happiness; in fact, it is the greatest hunger and desire of our lives. But we do not all agree on what happiness is. Why is this so? Most people agree that happiness is having what they want. But is this always true? Have you ever had what you wanted and still not been satisfied? Have there been times when everything seemed to work out for you, yet you still were not happy?

It sounds strange to say that happiness must be learned. It sounds even stranger to say that we may have to change some of the ways we think and act in order to be happy, but it is true. Many people are never happy because they never grow up. They are too self-centered and thoughtless to be happy, to achieve genuine joy. It takes wisdom and goodness to know where real happiness lies.

The greatest challenge of the moral life is to discover what real happiness is and to learn what we must do to have it. We spend a good part of our lives doing just this. We try our luck with all sorts of things that we think will make us happy. We explore and investigate. Sometimes we find happiness; sometimes we don't.

When we find true happiness, it can only be because we have learned to love the right things in the right way. That is why our searches for happiness always fail when we love wrong things or love good things in the wrong way. A happy person is not someone who denies the goodness of the world. A happy person knows how to love the good things of the world properly. Will loving your best friends make you happy? Yes, but only if you know how to love them. That is the whole point of the Christian moral life—learning to love all good things in all the right ways.

 What do you think is the key to finding happiness?

Happiness Needs

Ingredients for a Happy Life

If you were to make a list of everything you need for a happy life, what would it include? Take a minute to make that list now. Share it with someone.

What does our society tell us we need in order to be happy? A good way to answer this is to look through a popular magazine. Study the pictures and the advertisements. What messages about happiness do you see? Such magazines "preach a gospel" about happiness: We will be happy and satisfied if we look and dress a certain way, have lots of money, plenty of pleasures, a portion of power, and a taste of fame and glory. There is some truth to this because all these things are good and each contributes something to happiness. But is it the whole story?

Let's take a look at money, for example. Does happiness lie in riches? Many people think so. Money is one thing everybody wants, and hardly anyone ever thinks he or she has enough of it. Some people live as if it is money, not love, that counts and as if money is the one thing that will not let them down. Is this wrong?

Well, yes. Money is useful; there is no doubt about that. We need a certain amount of money to buy the things we must have to survive. But money is not enough to give us all the happiness we need. A person can have all the money in the world and still feel dissatisfied. That is because

wealth is not a powerful enough good to draw us more fully to life. Money cannot touch our hearts and satisfy our spirits. We need money to survive, but to love money as if it were the greatest good and the essence of happiness is both tragic and absurd. Think about it. To love money in this way makes money more important than we are.

The Pleasure Trap

If money alone can't lead us to happiness, what about seeking pleasure by itself? Since the days of ancient Greece, there have been people who believe that the highest good is pleasure and that pleasure is the key to happiness. These people were called *hedonists*, from the Greek word for pleasure. The hedonists believed that happiness was found in experiencing as much pleasure as possible. Although we seldom use this term today, there are a lot of hedonists around. They do everything they can to guarantee their comfort and pleasure. In this way they think they will be happy.

But they are terribly misguided because they love these good things in the wrong way. They are right that pleasures are good. But they are wrong when they dedicate their lives mainly to these things. For this is a false love, and false loves destroy us. The secret of happiness is to learn to love something that will bring us lasting joy. Money, pleasure, luxury, power, and fame can give temporary happiness. But if we have only these things and nothing more, we will lack the very thing on which human happiness most depends.

What is needed for a happy life? We are never too young to start answering this question. But we have to be careful; it is one of the most important questions we will ever ask.

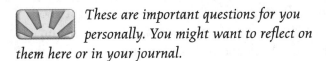 *These are important questions for you personally. You might want to reflect on them here or in your journal.*

Finding Happiness

Do we need God to be happy? Let's be honest about this: Many people would say no. God is not part of their lives, and they have no intention of inviting God in. They would not dream of connecting God with happiness. They do not think of God as a friend and certainly not as someone who loves them and gives them life. Rather, they see God as someone who is only concerned about laws.

Besides, such people believe they have found their happiness elsewhere. They look for all their happiness in, for example, sex, power, or money. Sometimes they look for happiness in alcohol and harmful drugs. And they are hardly ever alone because so many other people are searching for happiness in the same places. The only problem is that eventually they feel empty and alone and have to start searching for happiness all over again.

To what are we to give our hearts? When we learn the answer to this, we learn the meaning of happiness. But it is a challenging lesson to learn because there are so many conflicting messages all around us. Television and radio bombard us with messages about happiness. What about the music you like to listen to? What messages do the words give? We hear messages about happiness from our friends and our peers, from our families, and sometimes even from strangers. With so many people talking to us, to whom should we listen?

If we are Christians, we should listen first of all to Jesus. In one of the most famous passages of the Bible, the Sermon on the Mount, Jesus preaches about happiness. He gives us eight ways to happiness called the *Beatitudes*. His message may sound like strange music to our ears because he says that we will be happy if we are "poor in spirit," if we are meek and humble, if we are kind and merciful, if we seek justice and righteousness, and if, instead of causing hurt, confusion, and division, we are peacemakers (Matthew 5:1–10). In another famous passage Jesus tells us that we will be especially happy if we love God, with all our heart, with all our soul, and with all our mind and if we love our neighbors as ourselves (Matthew 22:37–39).

Is this the way we usually think about happiness? In fact Jesus' ideas are quite shocking. He does not say a word about sex or power or money or pleasure. He talks only about love and goodness and kindness and virtue. Not only does he tell us that these are what bring us happiness, but he also says that these are the very things that take us to God.

What does the Church have to say about all of this? The Church repeats this message of Jesus in every age. And the message is that we will find true and lasting happiness "in God alone, the source of every good and all love" (*Catechism*, 1723). Only in God is there the love and goodness we need to satisfy our hearts and fulfill our spirits.

Again, the question is: Do we need God in order to be happy? Some people may say no, but Jesus and his Church say that without God we cannot really be happy. God is our happiness because only in God will we find a goodness and love powerful and perfect enough to fill our hearts. Only God can heal our incompleteness and bring us peace and joy forever. Without God

in our lives every other good has no real meaning. Without God we cannot have real happiness.

 What about you? Do you feel that you need God to be happy?

A Covenant That Promises

Obeying someone else is probably the last thing you might think would make you happy. *Obedience* and *happiness* are not words that we normally link together. As Americans, we are much more likely to connect happiness with freedom and individual liberty.

But the ancient Israelites, our ancestors in faith, would have a few things to say to us on this subject. They were slaves toiling for the Egyptians, miserable in their slavery and desperately wanting to break free. Then God called Moses to lead them out of slavery and into the freedom of the promised land. Through the obedience of Moses and the people, what seemed impossible happened: God freed the Israelites from slavery.

Then God did something even more wonderful. God made a covenant with them. A *covenant* is a special agreement that binds a person or group to another person or group. It is an agreement in which each side promises something to the other.

CATHOLIC ID

Over 800 years ago, a woman was born who would help the world to understand what it means to be poor in spirit. Her name was Clare of Assisi. Today Catholics honor her as a saint. Why? Like Saint Francis, Clare, too, wanted to live the gospel life completely. For her that meant living like Christ, who had no worldly possessions. The example of her radical life of simplicity was so powerful that others joined her. She died in 1253, but her witness lives on in the religious order she founded, the Poor Clares. Today their example reminds us both to treasure the things of this world and to use them properly.

An example of a covenant is the vow a man and a woman make to each other in marriage. Their vow binds them together in love; each promises to support, care for, and be faithful to the other.

Sometimes a covenant is made even between unequals. This was the case with the covenant between God and Israel. God, the creator of the universe, chose the Israelites to be his special people on earth. God reached out to them in love and promised to watch over them, guide them, protect them from harm, and enrich them with all kinds of blessings. God told them, "Therefore, if you hearken to my voice and keep my covenant, you shall be my special possession, dearer to me than all other people, though all the earth is mine. You shall be to me a kingdom of priests, a holy nation" (Exodus 19:5–6).

A Covenant That Challenges

The covenant was not only a promise; it was a challenge as well. A covenant always carries expectations and obligations. Each side to the

sinai desert today

covenant has something to do, some special way to live. God promised to care for Israel and to keep Israel from harm. In return the Israelites had to promise God that they would obey his commandments and be faithful to him. In their obedience they would have true freedom.

Right after God called the Israelites to be his chosen people, he gave them the Ten Commandments (Exodus 20:1–17), the laws of the covenant. These laws were firmly founded upon the natural law. Revealed by God, they spelled out what the Israelites could and could not do if they were to remain God's special people. Their part in the covenant was to obey God and be faithful to whatever God asked of them. If they were faithful, they would enjoy the happiness and prosperity promised by God.

What does all this talk about covenants and commandments have to do with us today and with our happiness? *First,* by making a covenant with the Israelites, God was letting them know that their happiness and well-being depended on living in relationship with him. The closer they were to God, the happier they would be. The same is true for us. We are made for God, and we prosper and have life only when we live in friendship with him. Or to put it differently, we are happy when we love God.

Second, like the Israelites we find happiness when we are faithful to God and obey his laws. The Ten Commandments are designed, not to burden us, but to show us the shape that our lives must take if we are to be happy. We will find happiness when we honor God and love him wholeheartedly, when we respect our neighbors and treat them justly, when we tell the truth, and when our hearts are not ruled by jealousy and anger.

Third, the covenant and the commandments tell us that we will be happy when we choose goodness. Goodness and happiness go together. In fact we cannot be truly happy if we do not strive to be good. What the Israelites learned from experience we must learn, too. This is why Christians believe that a happy life is a life of goodness and virtue, never a life of wickedness and sin. It is also why obedience and happiness really do go together, especially when the one we are obeying is God.

Why do you think some people look for happiness in sex, power, money, music, alcohol, or drugs? What would you say to someone trying to find happiness in these things?

Look again at your list of the things you need to be happy. Do you still agree with it? Is there anything you would like to change?

My Thoughts...

Jesus' message about happiness is summarized best in his Sermon on the Mount, which is found in the Gospel of Matthew 5:1–10. Discuss this passage with some people in your parish. Do you agree with Jesus about what will make us happy?

YOU ARE MY WITNESSES

Scripture & My Life

In the Old Testament the Israelites were constantly warned about *idolatry*. To practice idolatry is to worship or adore something other than God. Like the Israelites, do we sometimes practice idolatry?

What are some idols in our world today?

Catholic Teachings

About the Ten Commandments

The Ten Commandments have always been a foundation and center for the moral teaching of the Catholic Church. The Church recognizes that the commandments express the most basic requirements of morality. They remind us of our relationship to God and teach us how we are to live together. The Church believes the Ten Commandments are something like a "recipe" for happiness because they list the rules we must follow in order to be happy.

CHAPTER 3

A Life of Discipleship

I will walk freely in an open space because I cherish your precepts.

Psalm 119:45

Every human life tells a story. Every life is an adventure with surprises and challenges, the ordinary and the unexpected, successes and setbacks. What kind of story are you hoping to "write"?

Your Story

Life is like a grand adventure story. It will take us places we never imagined we would be. It will challenge us in ways we could never dream. And if our lives are to be good stories, they will ask much of us. But they will also leave us happy and graced.

Sooner or later each of us asks this question: "How do I want to live my life?" This question is certainly worth considering because, even if we do not realize it, every day we are adding another page to the story of our life.

Already you have completed several chapters of your life story. How does your story read so far? Are you happy with it? Where is your story taking you?

How we answer these questions depends on how we envision our lives, what we are trying to accomplish, and especially, what kind of person each of us is trying to become right now.

Every human life tells a story. Some stories are beautiful and good. We see people who learn to be kind, who discover the meaning of love, who give of themselves, and who stay close to God. But other stories are sad. In these stories people never grow, never learn to give, never learn to love. They drift away from God and never find true happiness.

Perhaps the greatest challenge of morality is to find a story truly worthy of the gift of our lives. There are many stories being told in our world today that we should never embrace, stories that are boring, empty, and meaningless. What we need is a story that aspires to greatness, that will challenge us in every

24

possible way but that will also bring us a life of goodness and holiness. What we need is a grand adventure story guaranteed to change us in surprising but wonderful ways. As followers of Christ we believe we have found such a story. If we want to live the Christian moral life, the story of Jesus is the one we must make our own.

The Story of Jesus

We are Christians, not by fate or accident, but because we are convinced that in Christ there is life. We are Christians because we believe in our hearts that the most truthful and promising life possible for us is a life that follows Christ, learns from Christ, and imitates Christ in every possible way. We are Christians because we believe that following Christ will take us straight to God.

Listen to the very first words of Jesus in the Gospel of Mark. Jesus appears in Galilee and says, "This is the time of fulfillment. The kingdom of God is at hand. Repent, and believe in the gospel" (Mark 1:15). Jesus is saying to us, "Pay attention! Listen carefully! I have something fantastic and

wonderful to tell you. You can share in the very life of God if only you turn your hearts to me, learn from me, and follow me."

The word *gospel* means "good news," and indeed the gospel is the best possible news. Jesus pleads with us to "believe in the gospel" because the gospel shows us the path to life. We all come from God, and we must all find our way back to God. Jesus tells us he will show us the way. Jesus promises that if we follow him and make his life our own, we will enter the kingdom of God. Jesus is the way, the truth, and the life for us. We will not find life anywhere else. There is no other gospel, no other good news, no better story for us to live.

To learn and to live the story of Jesus is to begin a life of discipleship. A *disciple* is a pupil, a person committed to a special teacher, one who promises to teach important lessons about life. A disciple does not learn by sitting in a classroom. Instead, he or she learns by spending each day with the teacher, watching and carefully observing the teacher, listening to whatever the teacher says, and particularly, trying to follow the teacher's example. The gospels contain accounts of Jesus calling many

25

disciples to follow him. Jesus never told them exactly what to expect, but he did say that if they followed him, no matter how great the cost, they would have fullness of life. Jesus was very clear about what discipleship demanded. He told his followers, "If anyone wishes to come after me, he must deny himself and take up his cross daily and follow me" (Luke 9:23).

Jesus gives the same message to us who are his followers today. Our life of discipleship begins when we are baptized. Through Baptism we become the adopted sons and daughters of God and members of the Church. Baptism is the sacrament by which we are transformed into the likeness of Christ. Through God's grace we turn from sin and commit ourselves to Jesus for life. Baptism connects our lives to Christ forever. Our life is so completely linked to his that he is living in us and we are living in him. That is

why we say that in Baptism we "put on Christ" or are "clothed in Christ." With Baptism Jesus becomes for us not just a person to admire but the person who best represents what we want our life to be.

The heart of Catholic morality, then, is a life of discipleship, not laws and rules. It is a *personal relationship with Christ* that we try to deepen every day. Baptism gives every Christian the vocation of discipleship, the daily call to live in Christ, to learn from him, and to be his presence in the world. Thus, the Christian moral life begins with Baptism, is lived through discipleship, and ends when we reach the kingdom of God.

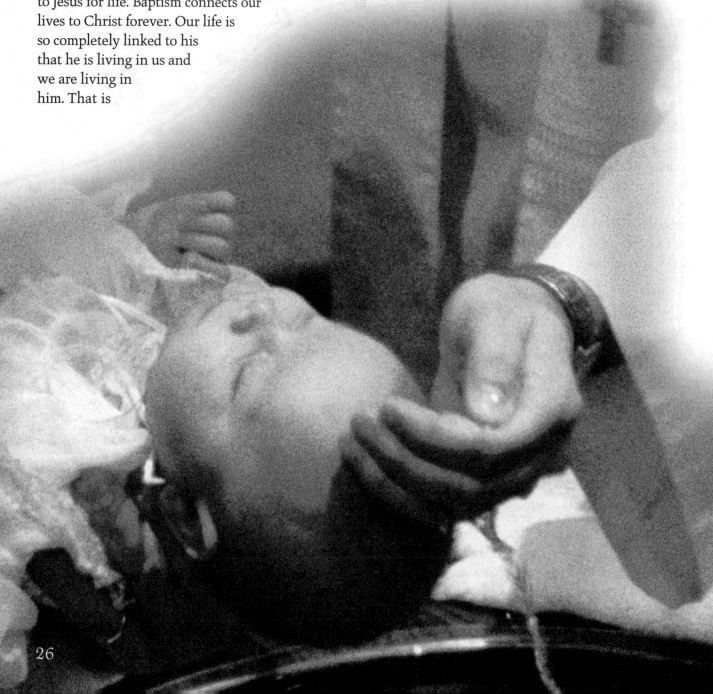

We do not live the story of discipleship by ourselves; we live it as members of the community of disciples we call the Church. When we are baptized, we are joined to Christ. We are also joined to a community of fellow believers who are trying to be the presence of Jesus to everyone they meet. One of the questions we should ask ourselves every day is this: How can I be Christ to each person I meet today?

Will people recognize Christ in me because I am just or kind or patient or forgiving? Choose one way you will deliberately try to be Christ to others today. Who knows? It might become a habit!

In Our Hands

The story of Jesus did not end when he left this earth. Just before he ascended to heaven, Jesus told his disciples, "Go, therefore, and make disciples of all nations, baptizing them in the name of the Father, and of the Son, and of the holy Spirit, teaching them to observe all that I have commanded you" (Matthew 28:19–20).

Those words were meant for all of us who are Jesus' disciples in the world today. As members of the Church, our special responsibility is to live the story of Jesus and be his witnesses to the world. We call this our mission. A *mission* is a special assignment a person is given to accomplish. The mission of every baptized Christian is to live the life of Christ in the world and to witness it to every person he or she meets.

One way to describe a disciple is someone who takes a chance with Jesus. This certainly seems to be true; in the gospels the disciples leave everything behind to follow Jesus for life. But it is also true that Jesus takes a chance with us because he puts the future of the gospel into our hands. That is a staggering thought: Jesus hands the gospel over to us and tells us to do something with it. He hopes that we will keep the gospel alive by sharing it with others, not bury it or leave it behind. It all depends on how we live. If the story of Jesus is not to die with us, we have to proclaim it every day by the way we live our lives.

A saint of the early Church said, "Let us, before all words, astound them by our way of life." All of us are called to astound people by the goodness of our lives. Can we do this? Can we really make a difference? Yes, we can. Acts of kindness, compassion, and forgiveness can put people in touch with the living Christ.

CATHOLIC ID

Baptism is the first sacrament. Through Baptism we are freed from original sin and any personal sins we may have committed and become children of God. We also become members of the Church, the body of Christ. The Church teaches that "for all the baptized, children or adults, faith must grow *after* Baptism. For this reason the Church celebrates each year at the Easter Vigil the renewal of baptismal promises" (*Catechism*, 1254).

Making a Difference

What was Jesus like? We see in the gospels that Jesus was faithful to God, hopeful, and loving. Jesus was compassionate, merciful, kind, just, truthful, and forgiving. More than anything Jesus saw each person as someone special, even those people whom others avoided. He always let them know that God loved them.

27

If we could always do the same, letting all whom we meet know that God loves them, what a fantastic difference we would make in our world! There would not be so many people who feel lost and lonely. Instead there would be a sense of joy, confidence, hope, and peace because people would be meeting Christ in one another.

There are many kinds of stories in our world, but as Christians we believe we have found the most beautiful, compelling, and wonderful story of all. We don't want to keep the story of Jesus to ourselves. Rather, we want to live in such a way that others will come to know it, too. This is exactly what it means to be a disciple.

Keeping the Story Alive

How can we best be the presence of Christ in the world today? How can we keep the story of Jesus alive? There are many ways, but the best and most important way to make Jesus' story our own is by not being afraid to love our neighbor.

But wait a minute. Why should we fear loving our neighbor? The answer is that it *sounds* easy, but in practice loving our neighbor is something that everyone finds a little difficult. It is easy enough to love our neighbor when we are allowed to decide who our neighbor is. Loving our neighbor is simple when the people we allow to be our neighbors are exactly like ourselves—people who look like us, act like us, and live like us.

Some people may find it more difficult to love their neighbors when they are different in some way, whether it is the color of their skin, their ethnic and cultural background, their physical appearance, their religious beliefs, their sexual orientation, or their talents. This is why we may be more likely to extend love of neighbor only to people with whom we are comfortable, people we find agreeable and compatible. Our love of neighbor may end when we meet someone who is not quite like us, who is "different."

If we are followers of Christ, we must do better. Our greatest moral responsibility is to love our neighbors as Christ loved them. Jesus never allows anyone to "play it safe." Indeed, Jesus always challenges us to practice the most radical and demanding love possible. To love our neighbor as Christians means that we are to love whomever God loves because God loves them. And God loves all people, even those we find most difficult to love. Jesus said we should even love our enemies. We are called to love everyone.

Someone once asked Jesus, "Who is my neighbor?" Jesus answered with one of the most powerful of his parables. Read Luke 10:30–37 to discover Jesus' answer.

Christ Healing the Blind Man, Nicolas Poussin, 1650

28

Things to SHARE

What kind of story do you want your life to tell?

The word *gospel* means "good news." In what way is the story of Jesus good news for you?

As Christians our mission in life is to keep the story of Jesus alive. How can you do this in practical ways in your own life?

My Thoughts…

OnLine WITH THE PARISH

We tell the story of Jesus when we love our neighbor every day. Think of some ways that you can practice love for neighbors in your parish. Can you volunteer to work in a food pantry or soup kitchen? Are there any elderly people you can visit? Are there younger children in school or in your family whom you can tutor?

YOU ARE MY WITNESSES

Scripture of My Life

There are many passages in the writings of Saint Paul in which he tells Christians that they are "the body of Christ" in the world. One example can be found in 1 Corinthians 12:12–30. Paul reminds the community that each has been entrusted with a special gift that will make Christ present to the world. His point is that Christ lives in the world through us. As the body of Christ, we are his "hands and heart" in the world.

What "special gift" do you have to offer?

Catholic Teachings

About Vocations

Each of us is called by God to serve him in a very special and personal way. This calling is our *vocation*. Our Christian moral life is lived out through our vocations. Traditionally, there are four vocations recognized by the Church: priesthood, religious life, marriage, and the single life. A vocation is not the same thing as a career. A career is something we choose as our work, but a vocation is a calling to a special way of life in loving service to God and God's people.

CHAPTER 4

Sin and Forgiveness

Peace I leave with you;
my peace I give you....
Do not let your hearts be
troubled or afraid.

John 14:27

Do you watch the evening news? Have you ever wondered why there seems to be so much bad news each day? How can God, who is so good, allow so much evil in the world?

And Now the News . . .

If you have asked questions like these, you are certainly not the first. Sometimes it seems as if the world is falling apart. Millions are starving in poorer countries because people in wealthier ones still have not learned to share. People are killed for a jacket or a pair of sneakers—and sometimes for no reason at all.

Sin. It is not the way life is supposed to be. But, as we read in the Genesis story, ever since the first human couple, perfectly safe and perfectly happy in the garden of Eden, chose to disobey God, sin has been part of life and part of each of us. If we are experts at anything, we are experts at sin.

In the Old Testament sin is considered as "missing the target" or "wandering from the path." Both phrases remind us that sin takes us in the wrong direction, that sin describes a life that has lost its way. If we constantly wander from the path, we will not only be lost; we will eventually destroy ourselves. Sometimes we meet people who are so involved with evil that they are really destroying themselves and do not know it. This is the real danger of sin: to get so caught up in the evil that we begin to destroy ourselves and have no idea that it is happening.

No matter how much we try to convince ourselves otherwise, doing evil never achieves good for ourselves or for anybody else. God never intended the world to know evil. God never desired killing and bloodshed, lies and falsehood, cruelty and thoughtlessness. God has a different dream for us. God's dream is that every human being and all of creation will know the fullness of life. God's dream is that we will live together in love, peace, and joy. When we sin, we reject God's dream and try to make a better dream of our own.

Sin never brings us that better dream. Sin never brings life; it never brings freedom or peace. The harvest of sin is always misery, hurt, and harm. It is not what God had in mind when he so carefully created the world. And it is certainly not what God had in mind when he fashioned us in love. In this chapter we will think about the meaning of sin and discover the only way out of it.

Sometimes the harm we do is terrible. We are not even sure why we do it, and usually we are unhappy after we have done it. But somehow we human beings persist in bringing more evil into the world. For instance, instead of using the gifts of speech and language to build people up, we use them to tear people down. We cause hurt with false rumors or tidbits of gossip. It gives us a sense of power and importance, but it wounds our victims, sometimes very badly. We may even allow a friendship to die because we are too proud to forgive or to be forgiven. None of this makes sense, but we do it all the time.

What's So Wrong with Sin?

If everybody is doing it, can it possibly be so bad? What's a little lying and cheating now and then, a little meanness and selfishness? Doesn't the good we do balance things out?

The trouble with thinking this way is that nobody is meant to be a sinner. This is the first problem about growing too comfortable with sin. To sin is to forget who we really are; it is a rejection of our true identity. Even though we have our faults and failings, the deep-down truth about us is that we are children of God. We are called to live in friendship with God and with one another.

To let sin take hold of our hearts is to take on a mistaken identity. It is to misunderstand who we really are. Sin is what happens when we forget who God calls us to be—the only creatures on earth who can know and love God freely and share in God's life completely. Every time we sin, we say no to God's way and to what God says will make us happy. When we sin, we make a mess of things.

Sin would not matter if there were nothing beautiful and graced in us that could be destroyed by it. Sin would not deserve a second thought if it did not terribly contradict the most wonderful truth about us: God loves us and wants to share his life with us. God wants us to find life through love, and sin says no to life and love. Sometimes sin disguises itself to look like life and love, but that is false. God is never false. God wants to share with us everything he has, and sin closes our hearts to his love.

A Dream Destroyed

Another problem with sin is that it rejects God's dream for the world. God wants us all to live together in justice, joy, and peace. God wants us to help one another and watch out for one another, not to hurt one another. God wants a world in which each person is actively concerned about every other person and all of creation. Just as sin is the way things are *not* supposed to be, this is the way they ought to be.

Sin wrecks things: life, the truth, property, a person's reputation, another person's heart. Take gossip, for example. It can seem so harmless, so natural. But gossip always does harm, however unintentional, because it invites people to think less of somebody else. Think about the obvious

33

example of war. War is sinful because war destroys everything: lives, families and friends, cities and towns, fields and rivers, and even hope. The evil of war is that it takes the creation God so carefully put together and deliberately rips it apart.

Finally, sin never brings us what we think it will bring. Every sin backfires. We lie because we fear what the truth might ask of us; we lie because we think lying will keep us free. But the more we lie, the more we become the sort of person whom nobody trusts. Sometimes we let jealousy and envy get the best of us, but this doesn't help either. If we spend all our time envying the talents of others, we never discover or develop our own.

If everybody is doing it, can sin be so bad? The answer, quite simply, is yes. Sin never brings joy; it brings only sadness and loss—to ourselves, to everyone around us, and to God.

Can you think of other examples of how people excuse sinful acts by calling them something different?

The Human Condition

How did sin enter our world? According to Genesis, the first book of the Bible, God created us to live in perfect happiness with him. But our first parents, called Adam and Eve, freely chose to disobey God. In doing so they fell away from the original state of happiness. The story of the fall of humanity is told in an unforgettable way in the third chapter of Genesis. There the inspired writers used rich symbols to bring out the truth that sin started with human beings, not with God. The garden, for example, was a symbol for the original happiness that God intended for us.

The truth for all time is told in the beautiful imagery of Genesis: Our first parents sinned. From that moment on they and their descendants (the whole human race) would know sickness and fear, confusion and pain, hard work and suffering, even death. Human beings were now flawed. We could still be good and know much happiness, but everything would be harder for us. We would all be afflicted with the same human weaknesses: pride, greed, envy, lust, gluttony, sloth, and anger.

This is our human condition. In so many ways we are good, but we are all too often sinners, too. We want to do what is right, but we can be petty and mean. We know we ought to tell the truth, but sometimes we lie. The words of Saint Paul ring true for all of us: "What I do, I do not understand. . . . For I do not do the good I want, but I do the evil I do not want" (Romans 7:15,19).

The sin of Adam and Eve is called *original sin*. It refers to the first sin of the human race. We are all born with original sin. It has been transmitted to us from our first parents and is therefore different from our personal sins. Original sin, then, is a state or condition into which we are born; it is not an act we personally commit.

Original sin explains why our human nature is weak, wounded, and in need of healing. We do not have to look far to see the effects of original sin in the world: war, hatred, racism, and violence of all kinds. No wonder we need Jesus to save us!

CATHOLIC ID

Did you know the Catholic Church teaches that besides Jesus there was one other person who never sinned? The Catholic teaching of the immaculate conception says that Mary, the mother of Jesus, was blessed by God so that from the very first moment of her existence, she was free from sin and full of grace. In 1854 Pope Pius IX declared this an official teaching of the Catholic Church. A feast commemorating the immaculate conception is celebrated each year on December 8.

Personal Sin

Even though we have been set free from original sin by Baptism, we still commit personal sin. The Church teaches that there are two kinds of personal sin: *mortal sin* and *venial sin*. As the name suggests, mortal sin is an act or deed that involves something so seriously evil that it brings death to the spirit of goodness in us and the divine life of the soul. Like a fatal wound, mortal sin kills God's life within us. The Church teaches that for a sin to be mortal, three conditions must be met:

• It must involve a grave and serious matter.

• We must have full knowledge that what we are doing is mortally sinful.

• We must freely and fully consent to it.

By contrast, venial sin names less serious sins. Venial sins weaken our life with God. Even though they do not destroy our life with God, they are still evil and should be avoided.

If we are wounded and weakened by sin, how are we to get better? What kind of medicine is there for this illness in our spirits?

First of all, there is *grace*. Grace is not something we earn or deserve. It is a share in God's own life. It is a gift of God's absolute goodness and mercy, which pardons our sins and heals us. Grace is forgiveness, freedom, and new life.

Our spirits are also healed from sin and strengthened in grace by the *sacraments*, especially Baptism, Confirmation, the Eucharist, and Reconciliation. Each is a way in which God gives us life through Christ so that we may grow in goodness and be ruled, not by sin, but by grace.

We will always struggle with sin and temptation. But we need to remember that grace is more powerful than sin and God's love and goodness are infinitely stronger than evil.

 What remedies do we have for the "illnesses" of our human nature?

A New Beginning

How do we deal with the mistakes and failures of our lives? If we have hurt a friend with a cruel remark, we have to do something or the friendship will be permanently damaged. If we have harmed another person's reputation with a lie, we have to find a way to deal with the damage done both to that person and to ourselves. If our sins are not to burden us forever, there must be a way we can recover from them. If we cannot erase the mistakes of our lives, can we ever be healed?

We can, but only if we risk forgiveness. Forgiveness is the only power we have against sin. The special power of forgiveness is that it frees us from the mistakes we have made so we can take up life again. To be forgiven is to be graced with the chance to leave our sins behind and begin again.

What if every wrong we ever committed could never be left behind but only carried forward? What if the unkind remark we made yesterday were to be added to unkind remarks we made last week and the week before? If this were the case, we could never be freed of our sins; we would carry to the future every sin we have ever committed. And we would be known not so much by the good we have done but by our mistakes. What a burden we would carry!

What kind of hope would we have if there were no such love as forgiveness? Life is a matter of going on together, and forgiveness is the love that makes this possible. The wonderful power of forgiveness is that it frees us from our mistakes and regrets so that we can look to tomorrow with hope.

Jesus and Forgiveness

Forgiving was at the heart of Jesus' ministry. The gospels can be read as true witnesses to the power of forgiveness. Forgiving sinners is what Jesus does more than anything else. There is, for example, the unforgettable story of Jesus encountering the woman who had been caught in adultery (John 8:3–11). She is about to be stoned to death by an angry crowd. But unlike the crowd, Jesus has no interest in condemning her. His sole desire is to forgive her. He tells her simply, "From now on do not sin any more."

Read through any of the gospels and pay attention to what Jesus does. He is always seeking out people who need to be forgiven. We find him at table with tax collectors, prostitutes, and people who have broken the law. Jesus is not afraid of them; he is there to forgive them. That is the heart of the gospel: Jesus comes, not to condemn sinners, but to call them back to life.

Jesus feels the same way about us. Jesus comes to restore us to health. Out of love he shared our human condition. Out of love he took on the sins of the whole world. Now the risen Christ heals our souls with grace, mercy, love, and forgiveness. He wants to restore everything that evil has destroyed.

Jesus heals us today through the sacraments, particularly through the sacrament of Reconciliation. The Church calls this a sacrament of healing because in this sacrament Christ, our redeemer, heals us from our sins and restores us to life. As in the gospel stories, Christ comes, not to condemn us or punish us, but to set us free so that we might turn from sin to goodness.

When we are forgiven, we ought to give thanks. And the best way for us to give thanks for having been forgiven is to forgive others. By doing so, we continue Jesus' ministry of forgiveness and reconciliation in the world, and we let God know we are grateful.

 Have you ever experienced a moment of true forgiveness? What was it like?

Describe sin in your own words. Where do you see sin alive in the world, both far away and close to home?

Do you agree that the result of sin is always sadness and misery, hurt and harm? Why or why not?

Why is it sometimes so hard to forgive?

My Thoughts…

Since all of us are members of a community, our sin never affects us alone; it damages and weakens a community as well, especially the community of faith. One way that our parishes acknowledge this is by holding Penance/Reconciliation services, particularly during Advent and Lent. As a sign of your membership in this community of faith, plan to attend the next Reconciliation service.

YOU ARE MY WITNESSES

Scripture My Life

Forgiveness is completed in reconciliation. To reconcile is to heal and restore relationships that have been damaged or broken by sin. One of the most famous and powerful stories of reconciliation in the Bible is the parable of the prodigal son (Luke 15:11–32).

Why does Jesus tell this story? What does the parable say about God? about forgiveness?

Catholic Teachings

About Sin

Original sin can be described as a "sickness of our spirits." We are not completely ill because of original sin, but neither are we completely healthy. Our human nature is a mix of health and illness. Our capacity to do good was certainly weakened and diminished by original sin, but it was not destroyed.

Finding True Freedom

My help comes from the LORD,
the maker of heaven and earth.

Psalm 121:2

What does freedom mean to you? Why is freedom so important to some people that they have been willing to die for it?

The Power of Freedom

You are at an age where freedom is very important, and it should be. You want freedom to explore life, to ask questions and make decisions, to think and to speak your mind. You want freedom to spread your wings, discover the wonder of yourself. Freedom is a great power, and we cannot live without it. But like any power it can be used well or poorly; it can give us life, or it can destroy us.

But what do we mean by freedom? For some people, the person who enjoys freedom is the one who is tied down by nothing, free from responsibilities. For others, true freedom comes with wealth and riches. But is freedom more than this? Does it need laws or rules? What does Jesus teach us about freedom?

Saint Paul wrote, "For freedom Christ set us free; so stand firm and do not submit again to the yoke of slavery" (Galatians 5:1). We should take these words to heart. Jesus did not come to free people from one thing only to enslave them with something else. Everything he did was intended to free people from whatever it was that oppressed them: sickness, injustice, hurts and disappointments, lack of self-respect, bad relationships, hopelessness.

And Christ wants freedom for us, too. A life in Christ *is* a life of freedom, a life that permits us the perfect liberty that we see in the lives of the saints, those people who freely did God's will all of the time.

The Truth About Freedom

But how can we be free if we are doing God's will? For most of us, doing someone else's will is exactly what we want to avoid. Jesus told his disciples that if they wanted to be free, they would have to deny themselves, take up a cross each day, and instead of going wherever they pleased, follow him wherever he took them. That hardly sounds like a life of freedom.

Generally, people think of freedom as freedom *from* something, especially freedom from restraints and restrictions. But as Catholics we think of freedom as freedom *for* something—freedom for service, compassion, justice, and love. We do not believe that freedom exists for its own sake, as if it were the most important value in life. No, we believe that freedom exists for the sake of something else: faithfulness, truthfulness, and especially love. We are most free when we do good for others, when we keep our promises, when we fulfill our obligations, and when we are kind.

Faith tells us that we are free when we live in a way that is

pleasing to God. Isn't this what we are saying in the Lord's Prayer when we pray, "Thy kingdom come, thy will be done on earth as it is in heaven"? These words remind us that we are most free, not when we are seeking our will, but when we are following God's. The prayer helps us to recall that our greatest liberty is in living, not for ourselves, but for God.

 What word or phrase comes to mind when you hear the word freedom?

The Importance of Conscience

Imagine this scene: You are shopping at a local mall with your friends. One of them decides that each of you should steal something from a store before you leave. It does not have to be expensive, but everyone has to take something. Your other friends agree to the plan. Now you have to make a decision. You want to tell your friends that what they plan to do is wrong, but you are afraid that they might turn against you or make fun of you. You do not want to lose them as your friends. You feel very uneasy. What should you do?

The "you" in the story knows what it is to have a conscience. That person is feeling the "pinch" of conscience, just as we do when we know that something wrong is about to happen and that we ought to do something about it. Our conscience will not leave us alone. It will trouble us until we do what we think is right.

Our conscience is one of the things that keeps us human, which is why it is important to develop our conscience as God wants, then listen to it and respect it. *Conscience* is the most basic awareness that some things are right and some things are wrong, and we need to know the difference and act accordingly. It is our "most secret core," where we are "alone with God whose voice echoes" within us (*Catechism*, 1776).

 Think of a time when you felt the "pinch" of conscience. What did you do about it?

A Precious Possession

Conscience also alerts us to the important goods and values of life and obliges us to respect them. It is our conscience that tells us that treating a classmate cruelly is wrong because every human being has dignity. It is our conscience that tells us that violence is evil, that suicide is a sin, and that justice is always important. Conscience is that special human capacity to know that morality matters in every area of life. In its most basic form, conscience lets us know that we should do good and avoid evil.

Does everyone have a conscience? Sometimes it seems not. Some people do terrible things and hardly seem bothered. They lie, they steal, they kill; they are cruel and treacherous, and yet they do not seem troubled at all by what they do. They feel no guilt, they show no sorrow or remorse; and if you tell them that they have done something evil, they laugh. How can people do terrible things and not be troubled? Have they lost their conscience?

We are all born with a conscience, but we can weaken and eventually destroy our conscience if we fail to take care of it or continually act against it. We care for our conscience when we do what is right; we destroy our conscience if we continually do what is wrong.

Conscience does not work the same way in everyone. Some people are more conscientious than others. Some have very sensitive and mature consciences, while the consciences of others are dull and undeveloped. Why is it that some people never lie because they know it is wrong and do not want to become liars, while others lie frequently and never give it a second thought? It is hard to say, but perhaps it is because some people are barely able to recognize right from wrong or even to realize that we ought to do what is right and avoid what is wrong. They do not recognize some of life's basic moral obligations—to be just, to be truthful, to respect another person's property.

Many things affect the development of our conscience for better or for worse: family background and upbringing, the choices and decisions we have made in the past, our temperament and personality, our friendships and the influence of our peers. These are the "facts" of our lives. We are lucky if we have been surrounded by good people who have shown us good example and helped us appreciate the difference between right and wrong. But there probably have been some people who have had a bad influence on us, who have encouraged us to do what is wrong and even to act against our conscience. These people claim to be our friends, but they really are not.

Conscience is one of our most precious possessions. We should guard it well because it is one of the most powerful signs that we are made in the image and likeness of God.

Following Our Conscience

The Catholic Church teaches that we must follow our conscience, but only after we have taken time to form our conscience. We should never act against our conscience because our conscience is our *self*. Our conscience is our moral dignity, it is our character, and it represents our integrity as persons created by God. To act against our conscience is to act against ourself. It is to say that we do not have the courage to be who we really are. This is why we feel bad when we do not do what our conscience tells us we ought to do. We not only let another person down; we also let ourself down because we have failed to be true to ourself.

It is necessary, however, to form our conscience so that it really can show us what we ought to do. If every person has the *right* to follow his or her conscience, every person also has the *responsibility* to educate it. A good conscience does not come naturally. It takes a lifetime

Can you think of someone who has helped you to know and choose what is good?

to form it. Our conscience must be educated so that it is able to recognize both what is good in a given situation and how we need to act in order to achieve it. To act in good conscience is, not to do whatever we want to do, but to do what we believe God is calling us to do.

Forming Our Conscience

How do we form our consciences responsibly? First, we need to listen to the important moral teachers in our lives. Jesus is our foremost teacher. He is the Word made flesh—the way, the truth, and the life. We hear his voice in the gospel; we listen as people of faith and are open to the guidance of the Holy Spirit, whom he sent to us.

Next we listen to the authority of the Church, whose teachings have guided us since the time of Christ and the apostles. In a special way, the pope and bishops teach us with the authority of Christ himself. This teaching authority in the Catholic Church is called the *magisterium*, from the Latin word meaning "teacher."

A very important role of the Church is to be a moral teacher about crucial questions of life. We need to know what the Church teaches about justice, respect for life, sex, ecology, drugs, suicide, and other moral questions. We need to listen to the Church's teaching, respect it, and let ourselves be challenged by it. Because it is guided by the Holy Spirit and founded on Christ, the Church is the only authentic teacher of faith and morals. This has been true since the time of the apostles. That is why we are called as Catholics to respond in faith and obedience to the Church's teachings. For in the Church we meet Christ and become his disciples.

We also must listen to our parents and teachers, family members we admire and respect, our pastors, and others whose goodness and wisdom we can trust. There is much that such people can teach us about what is right and wrong, about important moral values and principles, and about the way to make decisions when we are faced with difficult situations. They may not always tells us what we want to hear, but we should always listen to them carefully. They have our best interest at heart and can really help us.

Finally, in forming our conscience we should pray for the guidance of the Holy Spirit. Prayer is a very important part of educating our conscience in order to make responsible decisions. We should take time to speak to God about the decisions we need to make and the hard choices that we sometimes face. We should talk about our fears or uncertainties and ask the Spirit to guide us. When we pray, we invite God to be a "partner" in our decisions, which is tremendously reassuring. It lets us know that when we act in good conscience, we are never alone: God is always acting with us.

Face-to-Face with God

God is in love with us. Think about it. This is the God of the universe, the God who made the heavens and the earth, all the plants and animals, and every human being who has ever lived. God is in love with us. And he is waiting for our response. Will we love him or won't we? By the way we live our lives, we give our answer. That's what Catholic morality is all about.

When someone loves us, that person wants us to love him or her in return. It is the same with God. God will love us no matter what; but because God loves us, he cares what we do. God wants his love to be returned.

Our whole life can be seen as an open invitation to love God, who waits and hopes for our response. Isn't this how any friendship begins? Someone has to make the first move; someone has to extend an invitation. When someone invites us into friendship, that person waits for and hopes for our response.

As the *Catechism* reminds us, "God has loved us first" (2083). Throughout all of history God has invited every woman and every man to live in friendship with him. The stories of their lives have told and continue to tell of their response. Some love God dearly and faithfully. Some love God weakly and halfheartedly. And some never love God at all. If we realize how deeply and faithfully God loves us, how are we to respond?

Before we answer, there are two things we need to remember. First, we need to remember that God loves us first. We are here and created in God's own image because we are loved. Every human being is a personal expression of God's love. God has told us, "With age-old love I have loved you" (Jeremiah 31:3). God showed his love for the people of Israel by rescuing them from slavery and leading them to the promised land. God extended his love by sharing with us his only Son, Jesus, even to the point of his crucifixion and death. God continues to love by sending us the Holy Spirit; by coming to us in the sacraments; and by surprising us with acts of love each day in the goodness and kindness of others, in the beauty of nature, and in those quiet times when God speaks to us alone. As the prophets remind us, God's love is everlasting.

Second, we need to remember that there is only one God and that we are to love, worship, and serve this God. The first of the Ten Commandments proclaims this most basic truth of life: "I, the LORD, am your God…. You shall not have other gods besides me" (Exodus 20:2–3). In the Book of Deuteronomy, God speaks to the Israelites through Moses, telling them, "Hear, O Israel! The LORD is our God, the LORD alone! Therefore, you shall love the LORD, your God, with all your heart, and with all your soul and with all your strength" (Deuteronomy 6:4–5). And Jesus himself says, "The LORD, your God, shall you worship and him alone shall you serve" (Matthew 4:10). The message could not be clearer: There is one God in whom there is life and salvation. This God loves us faithfully and personally. We are to love and serve him in return.

That is why satanism is false and evil. *Satanism* is the worship and adoration of the devil, the one who is the essence of evil and hatred and death, the one who is hostile to God and everything that God wants. To practice satanism is to make our god the very one whose sole desire is to destroy us. If loving and serving God is a beautiful life, satanism is a perverted and evil one.

There is another danger known as the occult. Catholic moral teaching is critical of the occult and of *occultism*, which is an attempt to gain special knowledge or power over other people or events, usually through magic, astrology, or witchcraft. Occultism is dangerous because it is a sin against the faith, trust, and confidence we should have in God and that God alone deserves. We should love, serve, and honor God alone. We will not find life or freedom anywhere else.

 What do you think draws some young people to satanism or the occult?

Do you think every person has a conscience? Do you think that some people today have lost their conscience? Why?

Why is it sometimes hard to follow your conscience? What do you do when you find it difficult?

My Thoughts...

OnLine WITH THE PARISH

We celebrate the feasts of the saints throughout the year, commemorating them in our parishes at the Eucharist. The stories of the saints show us how different people have understood freedom and what they, such as Thomas More and others, have done with the gift of freedom. Read the life of your favorite saint. What does it tell you about his or her understanding of freedom?

YOU ARE MY WITNESSES

Scripture of My Life

The New Testament is quite clear on the subject of freedom. Saint Paul reminds us that if we turn away from Christ to sin, all of our freedom will be lost, and we will be slaves again (Romans 6:17–23). Jesus tells us that if we listen to him and follow his ways, we will know the truth and that the truth will set us free (John 8:32).

Did you ever think that there is a connection between truth and freedom? Think about it now and share your thoughts.

Catholic Teachings

About Conscience
Catholic moral teaching has always upheld the dignity of conscience. The Second Vatican Council declared that when we follow a well-formed conscience, we are truly trying to follow the will of God. The Church also reminds us that we have an obligation to follow an informed conscience. We cannot ignore it. In fact, when we listen to our conscience, we can "hear God speaking" (*Catechism*, 1777).

Have you ever thought of your conscience as "God speaking"?

CHAPTER 6

Finding the Sacred

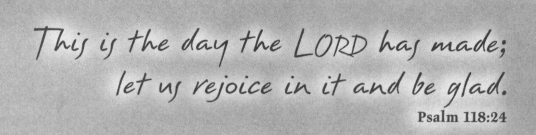

This is the day the LORD has made;
let us rejoice in it and be glad.

Psalm 118:24

People everywhere seem to be searching for meaning in their lives, for what is holy, what is sacred—really, for God. Are you on the same search? How do you go about it?

An Ongoing Conversation

What do you like to do most? Many of us like to spend time with friends. We enjoy the company of good friends because we can be ourselves with them. We want to be with our friends because we know that they care for us and are concerned about what happens to us.

What is true for our everyday friendships is also true for our friendship with God. We need to take time to be with God so that our friendship with him will grow strong. That is why prayer is a vital part of a life of friendship with God. In prayer we spend time with God. Like a best friend, God wants to know all about us. God wants to share in our lives completely because he loves us and wants what is best for us. God enjoys our company. He enjoys listening to us talk about what is happening in our lives. Like the best of friends, God rejoices with us when we are happy, celebrates with us when we succeed, and consoles us when we are sad.

Prayer is an ongoing conversation that we have with God. It is talking to God, but it is also listening to him. It is sharing our lives with God, but it is also letting God share his life with us. We see how important prayer is because Jesus prayed all the time, but especially at important moments of his life. He prayed before he called his first disciples to follow him. The night before he died, he prayed that he would have the faith and courage to do whatever God would ask of him. And when Jesus gave Peter a special role among the apostles, he prayed that Peter's faith would be strong and that Peter's love would be deep (Luke 22:32).

Among the Church's teachings on prayer are these three important ones:

- *It is always possible to pray.* Our whole life can be offered to God as a prayer. Prayer is listening to the Holy Spirit at every moment of the day. Prayer is openness of heart. It is remembering God's presence in our lives, and it is praising him by our actions.

- *Prayer is a vital necessity.* We cannot survive the setbacks and challenges of life if we are not close to God through prayer. And we cannot rejoice in God's love for us unless we take time to be with him and listen to him.

- *Prayer and Christian life are inseparable.* We cannot live the Christian life if there is no room for prayer in our day.

Our Father, who art in heaven, hallowed be thy name; thy kingdom come; thy will be done on earth as it is in heaven. Give us this day our daily bread; and forgive us our trespasses as we forgive those who trespass against us; and lead us not into temptation, but deliver us from evil. Amen.

The Prayer of Jesus

When Jesus' disciples asked him how to pray, he responded with the prayer that has become known as the Our Father, or the Lord's Prayer

(Matthew 6:9–13). This prayer is a kind of "outline" of the Catholic moral life. It makes it clear that we are sons and daughters of God in Christ. Like a loving father, God cares for us.

The Lord's Prayer also reminds us that God is all-holy and good and that God's goodness is beautiful. We are to grow in holiness and practice this goodness in our lives, always trying to do God's will. The Lord's Prayer encourages us to be bold in our prayers and never to be afraid to ask God for whatever we need most. Finally we are to ask God to keep us safe from all evil and harm and to "deliver us from temptation" so that we may always live in his love.

 Choose one phrase of the Our Father that means the most to you. Pray it silently now.

Powerful Language

Language—what power it possesses! We can use it well to compliment, to inspire, to forgive, and to love. We can use it to build others up, to encourage and support, to speak the truth, to correct or to console. We can use it to worship and to praise, to give thanks and to adore.

But we can also use language to hurt and to destroy. We abuse language when we use it sinfully to mock another person or lash out at another in rage. We use language sinfully whenever we lie or spread false rumors about others or curse them.

Language is so important that we can almost think of words as sacred. They are meant to bless. Sadly, though, we live in a world that seems unaware of this. We ourselves may even have lost the sense of language as a gift from God, a gift that we are to use to love and help and support one another. Listen to the way people talk to one another. Listen to the language of racism, the language of sexism. Listen to the cruel words spoken to gay men and women. We hear words that curse, words that wound, words that celebrate violence and death. The language of hate has become so common that hardly anyone notices.

How do the words you speak and listen to affect you? others?

God's Holy Name

The second commandment reads, "You shall not take the name of the LORD, your God, in vain" (Exodus 20:7). God is holy, and his name is sacred. We are to reverence God's name because it expresses who God is. We are to cherish the name of God and give it glory. We are to defend it and never profane it. To abuse God's name in speech is blasphemy. *Blasphemy* is a thought, word, or act making fun of or showing contempt or hatred for God, the Church and the saints, or sacred objects. Blasphemy is a very serious sin.

People also sin against the name of God when they lie under oath. When a person takes an oath—for example, in a courtroom—he or she swears that with God as witness, what he or she is about to say is true. God is invoked as a sign or a proof that every word that person utters is true. To lie under oath is to commit the sin of *perjury*. Perjury violates

the sacredness of God's name by calling on God to be witness to a lie.

Don't be confused. As we have just seen, *swearing* means taking an oath. It does not include vulgar language, which is simply crude and disgusting, but not sinful. People only show immaturity and ignorance when they use that behavior. *Cursing*, on the other hand, is sinful because it is calling on God to do harm to a person.

There are other ways that a person can violate the name of God. Sometimes when people make a promise, especially those most serious promises called *vows*, they call upon the name of God to witness their promise and to testify to the truth of their intentions. Couples do this when they exchange wedding vows. Religious priests, brothers, and sisters do this when they commit themselves to the religious life. It is fitting to invoke the presence of God at such moments. But we abuse the name of God if we use it to witness to a promise we have no intention of keeping.

How powerful human language is! How beautiful it can be—especially when it is used to praise and honor God's holy name.

 *Be very quiet. Slowly say God's name— "God," "Father," "Jesus," "Holy Spirit"— with great reverence.*

CATHOLIC ID

The Catholic Church is worldwide. There are Catholics in every country in the world. Perhaps someday you may have the opportunity to worship with Catholics from all parts of the globe at St. Peter's in Rome or at a World Youth Day. And that can be a powerful experience.

A Catholic's "normal" experience of Church, however, is the parish—the place in our neighborhood where we worship, celebrate the sacraments, and support one another with prayer and good works under the leadership of our pastor. Our parish is our "home" in the Church.

The Different Day

There was a time, not so long ago, when Sundays were different. Most people did not work or shop on Sundays. It was a day to slow down and rest, to relax with family and friends, to spend more time thinking about God. Sundays were usually quiet.

Perhaps this sounds so boring as to be almost frightening! What would we do if we actually had to stay home and spend the day with our families? Thank goodness that times have changed! Whoever thought Sundays should be different?

God did. It is his third commandment: "Remember to keep holy the sabbath day. Six days you may labor and do all your work, but the seventh day is the sabbath of the LORD, your God. No work may be done then" (Exodus 20:8–10). For the Jewish people the sabbath is celebrated on Saturdays. For Christians it is observed on Sundays as a way of commemorating the day of Jesus' resurrection. For both Jews and Christians the sabbath is a way of imitating and honoring God, who is described as doing the work of creation in six days, and resting on the seventh day.

For Catholics Sunday is the one day of the week that should be set aside for God. The primary way we do this is by joining our parish communities to celebrate the Eucharist. We are also mindful on Sundays of God's presence in our lives when we slow down and step away from our normal activities. By making Sundays different, we honor God as the creator and Lord of all life.

This sounds almost un-American! If there is anything Americans love to do, it is to make money. But there are more important things in life: time for rest and reflection, time to be with family and friends without having anything else to do or anywhere else to go, time for quiet and prayer, time to read and to think. If this sounds boring to some people, it may be because they look at life only in terms of work and activity. They have forgotton that there are other ways to live.

Jesus knew this. He kept the sabbath faithfully. We read in the gospel that he frequently felt the need to get away from the crowds, even from his work with people, to be alone with God. Often the crowds around him were so great that Jesus and the apostles did not even have time to eat. After an especially hectic time, Jesus said to his friends, "Come away by yourselves to a deserted place and rest a while." So they went off together in a boat to a quiet place (Mark 6:31–32).

Jesus invites us to do the same. "Come away," he says, "and rest a while." If we can learn to slow down at least one day of the week, we will discover some of the richest things in life: friendship, prayer, the company of people whom we love and who love us, and a little quiet and rest.

Sundays should be different. God thought it would be a good idea, important enough to make it one of the Ten Commandments. If it is good enough for God, maybe we should take the hint.

Do This in Memory of Me

From the very beginning of the Church, the followers of Jesus came together to remember and repeat what Jesus did at the Last Supper:

> Then [Jesus] took the bread, said the blessing, broke it, and gave it to [the apostles], saying, "This is my body, which will be given for you; do this in memory of me." And likewise the cup after they had eaten, saying, "This cup is the new covenant in my blood, which will be shed for you."
> Luke 22:19–20

Ever since the Last Supper, the Church has followed the command of Jesus to "do this in memory" of him. The Mass is the memorial of Christ's life, death, and resurrection. The early Christians celebrated this memorial on the first day of the week, Sunday, the day of Jesus' resurrection. From those very early days until now, the Church requires that all Catholics participate in the Mass on Sunday—or the evening before—to proclaim the mystery of Jesus until he comes again in glory.

Mass is another name for the celebration of the Eucharist. *Eucharist* comes from a Greek word meaning "to give thanks," and giving thanks is exactly what we do at Mass. We give thanks to God for all that he has done for us, especially for our salvation in Christ. In fact the risen Christ is with us as we celebrate. He told us, "Where two or three are gathered together in my name, there am I in the midst of them" (Matthew 18:20). How amazing this is! Jesus is with us as we remember and enter into the paschal mystery. Jesus is with us as we recall God's blessings to us through the ages and in our lives today. How can we not respond with thanks, adoration, and praise?

Perhaps some may be thinking of the Mass only as an obligation, as something we Catholics have to do. But it is so much more than that. It is a wonderful challenge to our faith. Do you remember the gospel account of John 6:1–15, in which Jesus multiplied the loaves and fishes to feed the hungry people? Well, there is a second part to that account.

The next day even larger crowds followed Jesus. He knew that they were looking for another miracle. He said to them, "I am the living bread that came down from heaven; whoever eats this bread will live forever; and the bread that I will give is my flesh for the life of the world" (John 6:51).

The people were astonished at his words, and disbelieving. "How can this man give us [his] flesh to eat?" they asked. Even some of Jesus' followers were surprised and wondered how anyone could take Jesus seriously. These disciples left him. Jesus asked the remaining disciples, "Do you also want to leave?" (John 6:67).

If there are times when you find the obligation of Mass hard to take, listen to Jesus' challenge. He asks each of us, "Do you believe in me? Do you love me? Will you stay with me?" Think of this the next time you do not feel like going to Mass.

When we respond to Jesus' challenge by participating in the Eucharist both as individuals and as a community and by receiving Jesus with reverence and faith, we grow as his followers. Jesus himself nourishes us in the Eucharist to live the moral life. We respond to Jesus as Peter did in the gospel: "Master, to whom shall we go? You have the words of eternal life" (John 6:68).

Plan a "different" Sunday for yourself with time for worship, rest, relaxation, and even quiet! What will you do?

How would you respond to this statement: "No one should celebrate Mass and remain the same"? Why or why not?

The next time you receive Holy Communion, what will you try to remember?

My Thoughts...

OnLine WITH THE PARISH

The Sunday Eucharist is the central activity of the community of faith. Let the Mass make a difference in your life by helping in its preparation. Work with a liturgy planning committee in your parish. Join the church choir. Look at the Sunday readings before going to Mass. Each of these activities is a way to deepen your participation in the Eucharist.

YOU ARE MY WITNESSES

Scripture of My Life

We were each baptized in the name of the Father and of the Son and of the Holy Spirit. Our name is a sign not only of our dignity and goodness as adopted sons and daughters of God but also of his presence in our lives. As Scripture testifies, "I have called you by name: you are mine" (Isaiah 43:1). Our name is also a symbol of ourself, which is why it should be shown respect.

Catholic Teachings

About Mass
The Eucharist is "the heart and the summit of the Church's life" (*Catechism*, 1407). For this reason the law of the Church says that on Sundays and other holy days of obligation, the faithful are bound to participate in the Mass. This law can also be satisfied when we participate at a Mass celebrated on the evening of the preceding day.

CHAPTER 7

Learning to Love

LORD, you have been our refuge through all generations.

Psalm 90:1

Home is the place where,
when you have to go there,
They have to take you in.

Robert Frost

What do you think Frost meant? Do you agree?
What would be your definition of home?

Ours for Life

Families are fascinating; no two are alike. Every family is full of characters, and the life of every family reads like a novel. All the stuff of life is packed into it: joy and tragedy, laughter and tears, great love and sometimes great hurt. Families teach us how to love, but sometimes they leave us feeling unloved. There may be days when we can't wait to go home, but there are also days when we think we will "die" if we can't get away.

Family life may not be perfect, but we need families. They help us to learn about life and about who we are. We need people around us who give us time to grow and time to make mistakes. There has to be some place where we feel we belong and are at home. Most important, there have to be people who will accept us, love us, and forgive us no matter what, simply because we are theirs and they are ours.

Most of the time we are part of families that are a mix of good and bad, often happy, basically healthy, occasionally troubled. There are strains and hardships as well as comforts and supports in all families. There are great challenges and great changes. And sometimes there are moments when everything seems to be falling apart. When this happens, family members are challenged to rediscover the love they have for one another, to support one another, and to ask God's help to see them through tough times.

Some children may live with only one parent. Some may have no idea where or even who their fathers or mothers are. Sometimes a parent may abandon the family, which is a terrible thing and a loss that can stay with one for life. This is not the fault of the children. They should never feel guilty, nor should they be blamed.

Some families break down when parents separate or divorce, and the separation can be very difficult. Sometimes parents stay together but are wounded by problems such as alcoholism or abusive behavior. When situations like this occur, young people should never blame themselves. They should look for help from trusted adults.

Families are meant to be a great gift of our lives. In families we should come to know God and his love for us. In families we learn about life and about ourselves; we grow and develop the talents and skills that we will need for life.

 Make a list of ways in which you have been "shaped" by your family.

Families Matter

One of the most important roles of the family is to educate us in the values and virtues that we need in order to move out into the world and live peaceably with others. Family life should prepare us for life in society, in the wider human community. It should teach us how to live in a way that is good both for ourselves and for others. We have to learn this somewhere if we are not to make a mess of our lives and our world. The most fitting place for this education to occur is within the family.

A healthy family life teaches us the importance of sharing and cooperation; it teaches us how to care for others and be concerned for their happiness. It shows us how to be faithful to others and to our promises. Family life should also show us how to deal with differences constructively instead of violently, a skill that is greatly needed in our world today.

It is clear, then, that good family life is crucial to the well-being of the whole human family. A family is like a miniature community. It is built around common values, beliefs, and goals. It prospers only when each member watches out for the well-being of every other member, when every member respects the dignity of the others.

 What basic skills for a happy life have you learned from your family?

Love and Justice

Of all the virtues and skills good family life should teach us, two of the most important are love and justice.

Love We have to learn how to love if we are to have good friendships today and good marriages later in life. When young adults leave home to take up life on their own, they need to be people who know how to love and to be loved. They need to have an understanding of all the many characteristics of love: openness, affection, acceptance, care, faithfulness, patience, and forgiveness. Love is made up of all these things, and people who love know when and how to use them.

Justice Justice is the virtue that reminds us that we are both connected to others and responsible for them. Do you remember the story of Cain and Abel in Genesis? God, knowing that Cain had killed his brother Abel, asked him, "Where is your brother Abel?" Cain, trying to fool God (always a bad idea!), answered, "I do not know. Am I my brother's keeper?" (Genesis 4:9). The answer, of course, is yes. We are our sisters' and brothers' keepers; we are responsible to one another and have obligations to one another.

It is important to remember that we are not merely individuals, that we are also part of larger communities: churches, neighborhoods, nations, the world, the universe. We are related to every human being and all of creation because all of us are members of the family of God.

The Church teaches us that "family life is an initiation into life in society" (*Catechism*, 2207). Life in our family teaches us what we need to know to live well with others. This is why families matter.

Respect and Gratitude

Do you always understand your parents? Do they always understand you? What do you think makes understanding difficult sometimes?

CATHOLIC ID
Parenting and family life are two of the most important moral issues we will ever have to face. They affect us each day. In fact, these may be part of your future vocation. And what is the family? Here are the thoughts of Pope John Paul II: "The family, which is founded and given life by love, is a community of persons: of husband and wife, of parents and children, of relatives" (*Apostolic Exhortation on the Family*).

Perhaps you had a misunderstanding with your parents as recently as yesterday. Maybe you will have another one tomorrow. Misunderstandings are to be expected as you enter adolescence. Adolescence literally means "growing into adulthood." It is the time of your life when you are poised between childhood and adulthood. The hard part about adolescence is that you are no longer a child but you are not quite an adult either. You probably no longer accept something just because an adult tells you to, and sometimes you may even reject something just because an adult tells you to accept it. Adolescence is a time when you are expected to change and to develop. That is why it is normal for adolescents to be both confident and a little confused. Because Jesus also went through adolescence he understands the challenges you face at this time of your life.

This is all part of coming to know yourself and trying to take charge of your life. You begin to question, to wonder, and to doubt. You aren't so sure about things that you once took for granted. You want to choose your own values and make your own decisions. You want freedom to explore the world on your own. This is the time of life when your ties to home are stretched. You move farther away, but something still pulls you back. You want more independence, but you also want the security of home.

Amid all this change, discovery, confusion, and transition, you are supposed to "honor your father and your mother" (Exodus 20:12). This is the fourth of the Ten Commandments. In general the fourth commandment requires that we honor and respect all our neighbors, and every human being is our neighbor. But no "neighbor" is closer to us than our own parents. Perhaps some of us were cared for by foster parents or adoptive parents. Whoever has loved us, watched over us, and taught us about life and about God is the "mother" or "father" we are meant to honor.

What can we give our parents in return for all that they have given us? There are some debts we can never repay, and our debt to our parents is one of them. But we can show that we are

grateful. We do this when we love and respect our parents, listen to them, and obey them. This does not mean that we must always agree with our parents, and it certainly does not mean that we will always want to do what they ask of us. It does mean that we obey our parents not only as a sign of our respect and love but also because we know that they truly care for us and want what is best for us.

The only exception to our obligation to obey our parents is if they should ask us to do something immoral or something that we sincerely feel would violate our conscience. Obedience should never be blind obedience. In fact the word *obedience* really means "to listen."

The obligation to obey our parents ceases when we reach adulthood and leave home; however, the duty to respect our parents never ends. We have responsibilities toward our parents as they grow into old age. We fulfill these responsibilities through our friendship with them, by financial support if it is needed, and by helping them with things that they are no longer physically able to do.

Parents also have duties toward their children. The Church teaches that parents must think of their children as God's children, too, and as persons deserving of respect. Parents should create a home where there is love, tenderness, and support. Parents are responsible for the moral education of their children, especially in the virtues and in the true meaning of freedom and love. Catholic parents are called to be their child's first teachers in the faith.

Think of some of the most important things you have learned from a parent about your Catholic faith. Name three of them.

Rules and Responsibilities

What would the world be like if there were no people in charge? Suppose there were no president to lead us, no congress to make laws, no courts to administer justice. Suppose there were no pope or bishops in the Church, no teachers, no police. What if no one had authority over anyone else, if there were no one to rule and therefore no one to obey?

Sound great? Not really. Whatever measure of freedom we might enjoy in such a world would be overwhelmed by the chaos that would surely follow. A world without people in positions of

59

leadership is a world that will quickly fall apart. As much as we may dislike having people to whom we must answer, we need someone in authority.

The fourth commandment calls us to respect not only our parents but also all those who, for our own good, have legitimate authority over us. This includes other relatives, such as our grandparents and aunts and uncles; but it also includes our teachers; the priests and sisters in our parishes; the pope, the bishops, other leaders in the Church; and our government officials, including all those in law enforcement.

To respect these people because of their position does not mean that we must agree with everything they say or do. It does mean that we must recognize and appreciate the authority and responsibility that come with their positions. Society, like a family, is held together by respect. If citizens of a country or community or members of a church lose respect for those in authority, that country, community, or church will soon fall apart. The same thing happens in a school. If students show no respect for their teachers or if teachers show none for their students, the school falls apart.

Of course respect must be earned. Persons in authority must remember that their authority is given for service, not for personal gain or power. The real purpose of authority is to bring about justice: to make sure that the basic needs and fundamental rights of all citizens are respected, to ensure social order and harmony, and to preserve the peace.

Government also has responsibilities to families. If individual families, because of unemployment or insufficient income, cannot provide for themselves, government has a moral responsibility to see that their basic needs are met. At the same time government must not interfere with a parent's right to bring up children according to his or her own moral and religious beliefs.

Just as those in civil authority have obligations to citizens, we as citizens have responsibilities to the community. Our primary responsibility is to be good citizens, which means that we should obey the laws, show respect and tolerance toward others, treat people justly, and be informed about the issues and challenges that face our community. As we grow older, responsible citizenship includes paying taxes, exercising the right to vote, and serving on juries. All these duties and obligations are vital to *patriotism*, the virtue by which we show love and support for our country and strive to be responsible citizens.

 Give examples of what is meant by good citizenship and patriotism.

60

How does family life teach us about love? How does it educate us about justice?

What are some of the problems and challenges facing families today?

We are told by the fourth commandment to honor our father and our mother. What does this mean for you?

My Thoughts…

OnLine WITH THE PARISH

Our involvement in the parish is important because it reminds us that in addition to our immediate family, we are also members of God's family. Every person in the parish is a sister or brother to us, not by blood, but by Baptism. The next time you are at Mass in your parish, say a prayer for all of the members of your parish, your "family of faith." Think about your own immediate family as part of this great family of the people of God.

YOU ARE MY WITNESSES

Scripture of My Life

The Ten Commandments are also known as the *Decalogue*, from a term that literally means "ten words" or "ten sayings." The first three commandments focus on our relationship with God and the love and honor that we owe him. Commandments four through ten focus on the honor and respect that we owe our neighbors. Take some time to read and reflect on the Decalogue (Exodus 20:2–17).

The Ten Commandments are listed in the back of this book. Learn them by heart.

Catholic Teachings

About Civil Authority

In April 1963, Pope John XXIII issued an encyclical, an important letter to the whole Church, entitled *Peace on Earth*. In this letter he said that all true authority comes from God and that therefore those in authority are accountable to God and must respect the moral order established by him. The pope said that government leaders exercise authority rightly only when they use it to achieve justice and the common good.

CHAPTER 8

Choosing Life

*I came so that
they might have life
and have it more abundantly.*

John 10:10

What do you think of when you hear the word peacemaker? Do you think of someone who is weak or strong?

The Work of Peacemaking

No one could accuse Jesus of being weak, but he was not afraid to be a peacemaker. He asked his disciples to turn the other cheek and to love their enemies (Matthew 5:39, 44). Even as he was being arrested, he told the hotheaded apostle Peter to put his sword away, "for all who take the sword will perish by the sword" (Matthew 26:52).

Jesus tells us that his disciples seek peace. They do not hate; they do not choose violence as a way of settling differences. They absolutely refuse to murder, whether with weapons or with words. Modeling themselves on Jesus, who died that all might live, they bring peace to the world.

Sometimes it seems that peace is hard to find in our everyday life. People seem quick to take offense and eager to seek revenge. People are gunned down randomly—because someone wants their jacket, because they cut someone off in traffic, because they look at someone the wrong way.

Who says life is sacred? Everywhere we look, we see attitudes and actions that say that life is cheap and meaningless. If ever the world needed peacemakers, it is now.

Choose Life

The fifth commandment is "You shall not kill" (Exodus 20:13). It is simple, direct, and absolutely clear. All life depends on it. Forget this commandment, and death takes over. Without a good understanding of what the fifth commandment means, it is easy to become a killer.

Think of the story of Cain and Abel, the first brothers. Cain was resentful that Abel's offering was more pleasing to God than his own.

And in the blink of an eye, blood was shed as one brother murdered the other (Genesis 4:3–8). Since that day God's gift of life has often been met with violence.

The only way to break the cycle of violence is to look to Jesus and to refuse to accept the belief that violence is the way to settle differences. The fifth commandment teaches us that violence is never the answer. Revenge never makes things better. That is why Jesus told his disciples to love their enemies instead of destroying them. As usual some may think that Jesus was asking too much. But true peacemakers know that Jesus shows us the only way to stop the violence. Blessed are the peacemakers. They are not weak but strong. They are the true followers of Jesus.

Have you ever "turned the other cheek" instead of trying to get revenge? Share your experience.

LIFE A WONDERFUL CHOICE CATHOLIC PARISHES

The Gift of Life

God alone is the Lord of life. What does this mean? It means that because we cannot give life, we are not supposed to take life. Life is a gift from God. It is God alone who creates; he alone brings to life every woman and every man.

Human beings do not create life; we are entrusted with life. God calls us to love, care for, and protect all life because life ultimately belongs, not to us, but to God the creator.

Unfortunately some people do not remember or believe this truth. They act as if life belongs to them. They act as if they, not God, were the lords of life and could do as they wish with any life—their own, another's, even those of animals.

But what does such an attitude say about the unborn child, who cannot defend itself? What does it say about people with mental or physical disabilities, people who need special care and loving attention? And what does it say about the old and infirm, who need to feel they are wanted and loved?

It is all a question of vision. The fifth commandment forbids direct and intentional killings as gravely sinful. Killing is direct and intentional when its purpose is to take the life of another. If a person kills in self-defense, the act is not murder because the primary intention of the act is to defend one's own life, not to take the life of another. Even in self-defense, however, we should not use more force

than is necessary to protect ourselves. Killing in self-defense is not justified unless it is the only way to protect ourselves from someone intent on doing us serious harm.

From Beginning to End

Even though abortion is legal in the United States, the debate over it rages on. Those favoring the right to abortion argue that it is a matter of freedom of choice. According to this view a woman has a right over her body, and the question of abortion is a private and personal matter with which no one else can legitimately interfere.

The Church teaches that abortion is a question, not of individual rights or personal freedom, but of unjustly taking the life of an unborn child, who from the first moment of existence "must be recognized as having the rights of a person" (*Catechism*, 2270). More important than individual freedom is our

personal responsibility to care for and protect the unborn child, who cannot speak for or defend itself.

Just as the Church calls us to respect life at its beginning, it calls us also to respect life as it nears an end. The Church condemns euthanasia. *Euthanasia* is the act of intentionally bringing about the death of one who is gravely ill. Its purpose is to relieve a person of intense suffering. However, because euthanasia deliberately takes the life of another, it is morally wrong.

The Church clearly teaches that we must take all *ordinary means* to preserve human life. However, it does not teach that life ought to be preserved at any cost. The Church teaches that *extraordinary means* need not be used to preserve the life of someone who clearly cannot survive. This means that there is no moral obligation to use medical procedures that are very expensive and unusual if their effect is simply to delay death rather than restore life. Even so, when a person cannot be cured and is facing death, we stand by that person, pray for and continue to love that person, and offer whatever care and consolation we can. In this way we show our respect for the dignity of the person and our hope in the resurrection.

The Challenge to Love Ourselves

Do you love yourself? Do not be so sure that you do. Most people do not love themselves, at least not in the way they should. Why is this so? Perhaps we have a poor self-image. We may not recognize our gifts and our talents. Whatever the reason, it seems that many people are not very good at loving themselves.

Our faith tells us the opposite. Our life is a gift from God. God wants us to love ourselves. Jesus said that we cannot really love another person, or even God, if we do not also love ourselves.

The fifth commandment forbids unjustified killing of ourselves. To harm oneself is not to love oneself, and it certainly is a lack of gratitude for God's gift of life. The fifth commandment obliges us to take care of ourselves and to look after our health by eating properly and getting enough rest and exercise. It also obliges us to avoid harmful and destructive behavior with substances such as alcohol, tobacco, and drugs.

Care for our physical, emotional, and spiritual health is essential. If people ever find themselves in an abusive situation, including physical or sexual abuse, they should seek whatever help they need to get out of that situation immediately. Victims of abuse should never be afraid to seek help.

Although it may be hard to admit, some "friendships" can be unhealthy. An example of this kind of unhealthy relationship is a gang. A gang can seem to provide ready-made friendships; it may even seem like a family and give one a sense of identity. But any person or any group that pressures us to do what is wrong—to deal in drugs, to be violent, even to commit murder—are sinning against us; and if we stay with them, we are sinning against ourselves.

 Think about your friendships right now. Do they help you to "choose life"? How?

A Healthy Love of Self

Having a healthy love of self can be tough at times. We have bad days. Perhaps we do not do as well on a test as we expected, or we feel a little lonely or misunderstood. These are real feelings. But we should not let such feelings control our lives. We should resist them, fight them. When we find, however, that we cannot overcome feelings of sadness and depression, a healthy love of self demands that we get professional help.

Unfortunately some people look for help in the wrong places. No matter what television ads may say, alcohol, drugs, and tobacco will not make us "cool" or solve our problems; they will just create new ones. When people are addicted to alcohol or drugs, life passes them by. The truth is that drugs become our masters and we their slaves.

The ultimate act of self-hatred and despair is suicide. People who take their own lives do not love themselves. There is no more unnatural act than suicide. The most basic human instinct is to preserve life, not destroy it. There also is no more unloving act, since by taking our own life, we turn away from the love that others, especially God, have for us. And to assist another person in committing suicide is not an act of friendship or support. Rather, it shows a terrible lack of love and is a horrible evil.

Life is too wonderful, too full of possibility to throw away. This is true even on days when it's hard to believe. Believe it! Choose life.

 Did you ever think that being a responsible Catholic has anything to do with the way a person drives a car, a boat, or an airplane? It does. People seriously violate the fifth commandment "who, by drunkenness or a love of speed, endanger their own and others' safety on the road, at sea, or in the air" (*Catechism,* 2290).

Breaking the Cycle

Was Jesus being foolish when he told us to love our enemies? No. The power of Christ is a power for healing and peace. Too many people choose to practice another kind of power—the power of anger and hate. Of course anger is not always a sin; in fact it can at times be very healthy. We should be angry when people hurt us, treat us unjustly, or ridicule us.

Healthy anger is a sign of healthy self-love. But anger becomes unhealthy and sinful when it grows into a desire for revenge and leads us to want to do harm to those who have hurt us.

Anger becomes especially destructive when it turns into hatred. Hatred may destroy the person we hate, but it always harms ourselves. Hatred is like a poison in our hearts. If we become people who hate, we can be sure that we will add to the misery of the world.

Wars start because of anger and hate. There is no more vicious power. Wars destroy everything and seldom settle anything. All that wars do is plant seeds for future bloodshed. There is no more obvious violation of the fifth commandment.

Finally there is the question of capital punishment, the practice of putting criminals to death for certain crimes. This is an issue over which people remain deeply divided. How should we as Catholics respond?

There is no easy answer. Those who support capital punishment argue that certain crimes are so terrible that nothing less than executing the criminal will satisfy justice. Furthermore they say that the state has a responsibility to protect the safety, freedom, and peace of its citizens. Opponents of capital punishment argue, however, that executing criminals does not prevent crime. Many also argue that the majority of those executed are poor and uneducated persons who cannot afford expert legal advice. The Church allows for the death penalty only in cases of extreme gravity, which means very rarely, if ever.

God says to us: "Choose life" (Deuteronomy 30:19). How can you choose life right now?

68

Should we take Jesus seriously when he tells us to love our enemies? What do you think would happen if we did?

Why do you think there is so much violence in our world today? Why do people find it hard to live together in peace?

My Thoughts…

OnLine WITH THE PARISH

Jesus tells us that before we bring our "gift to the altar," we should be reconciled with anyone with whom we might be angry or anyone we need to forgive or from whom we need to seek forgiveness (Matthew 5:23–24). We should not approach the altar to receive Communion if we are not at peace with our sisters and brothers. If there is someone with whom you must be reconciled, talk to that person and try to settle your differences before you next go to Mass.

YOU ARE MY WITNESSES

Scripture of My Life

One short verse from the Gospel of John tells it all: "And the Word became flesh and made his dwelling among us" (John 1:14). What greater evidence can we find to remind us that human life is sacred? After all the Son of God became one of us at the incarnation. If God thinks that human life is so important, shouldn't we think so, too?

Catholic Teachings

About Scandal

The Church teaches that "scandal is an attitude or behavior which leads another to do evil" (*Catechism*, 2284) Friends have tremendous influence over one another. When we use our power and influence to persuade others to do wrong, instead of urging them to do what is right, we are guilty of the sin of scandal. We show ourselves to be an enemy rather than a friend.

Loving for Life

CHAPTER 9

My heart and flesh cry out
for the living God.

Psalm 84:3

*Everybody is interested in sex, and it shows.
Sex is in our music; it's in the clothes we wear and the way
we talk. It's in almost every movie and all over TV. There's hardly
a day that goes by when it isn't on our minds as well.
Why do you think sex sells?*

Sex: A Gift and a Blessing

Watch the commercials on television, or flip through a magazine. Sex is used to sell cars, clothes, toothpaste, perfume, music, and even food. You can get the impression that, more than anything else, sex moves the world and keeps us going. Sex must be pretty great.

And it is. Sex is a gift and a blessing. God made it a powerful part of us so that the human race would continue and thrive. There is nothing evil or disgusting about sex in itself. God did not create sex to test us, tempt us, or mess us up. Our sexuality goes to the heart of who we are. We cannot help but be sexual. We have bodies, feelings, and sensations, and we are made to be attracted to somebody else. It is all part of God's plan. That is the point: God made us sexual in order to bring us together.

The whole point of sex is to share our love responsibly and with commitment; the point of sex is love. God gave us our sexuality—male and female—to bring new life into the world and to teach us how to love. He gave us sexuality so that we might learn something about higher values in life, such as true and lasting friendship, genuine intimacy, and trust. God also warned us of the dangers of forgetting these values. We learn in the sixth and ninth commandments: "You shall not commit adultery," and "You shall not covet your neighbor's wife" (Exodus 20:14, 17).

The message we constantly hear is that sex is natural, and it is. But what is meant by this is that sex is purely biological, no different from eating when we are hungry, drinking when we are thirsty, or sleeping when we are tired. We reach a certain age, and our bodies start to change. Our glands and hormones get to work, and we find ourselves attracted to others. We get an urge, and we answer it. It sounds rather crude, but that is the message of much of our music and many of our movies. It's simple biology. What do you think?

The Church reminds us that when we treat sex this way, it loses its beauty, grace, and deeper meaning. If sex is only biological, then human beings making love are no different from animals. If that's all sex is, it would be missing something essential. What makes sex beautiful and wonderful is that it is also spiritual. Sex is intended to involve our hearts and souls, not just our bodies.

Sex is fascinating and powerful because it involves our spirits as much as our bodies. It is through sex that two people can come to know the mystery of each other and become one. But this takes a commitment to a lifetime of faithful, trusting love, not just a brief experience of physical pleasure.

God meant us to use the gift of sex to learn what it means to love faithfully. Anybody can engage in sexual activity; it does not take much intelligence or skill. The real achievement is to learn how to love generously, faithfully, and completely.

From Revolution to Reality

For years now there has been talk about the "sexual revolution." This is the idea that says we are free to use sex any time and any way we want. The message of this revolution is that any sexual activity is healthy, normal, and a strictly personal choice. The "revolution" tells us that sex is the source of happiness and the key to fulfillment. So if we are not engaging in sexual activities, according to popular opinion, we are not really normal, and we cannot possibly be having much fun.

CATHOLIC ID

Many young Catholics are taking a stand for chastity and against sexual activity before marriage. In their parishes they are publicly promising to abstain from having sex until marriage. This is a very courageous thing to do.

This popular opinion has led many to believe that sex really is a matter of private, individual judgment, unrelated to moral values. And here are some of the results:

• soaring divorce rates
• millions of babies born outside of marriage
• skyrocketing teenage pregnancies
• rapidly increasing numbers of abortions
• a growth in sexually transmitted diseases.

Surely these are clear signs that the "revolution" has been a failure and that a permissive, "anything goes" attitude can never bring happiness. How happy is a teenage girl who is pregnant but abandoned by her boyfriend? How happy is a teenage boy who is pressured by his friends to have sex because "everybody is doing it" and because he doesn't want to feel "weird"? And how happy is the beautiful young person whose promising life is cut short by AIDS?

Sexual activity without deep, faithful love is empty. Sex without faithful, mature love is pure selfishness; and selfish love wounds people with lies, deception, and betrayal. Too many people have learned this the hard way. No matter how hard we may try, we can never keep sex simply physical. Sex is an act that involves the *whole person* in a way that no other act can. Sex involves not just our bodies but our minds and feelings and our souls as well. This means that if you give yourself completely to someone with your body, you must be prepared to give that person your heart and soul, too.

That is why the Catholic Church teaches that certain kinds of sexual activities are immoral and sinful. The chart on page 74 describes some sins against the sixth and ninth commandments.

Perhaps you are wondering why the Church has so much to say about sex. Isn't sex a personal choice? The obvious answer is that sexuality involves more than our personal life. The gift of sex is given so that two people can become one in love and that the natural outcome of this responsible and faithful love is new life—children. That is why sexuality is a moral issue. It has to do with values that make a

Understanding More About Sexuality		
	Meaning	*Why It Is Sinful*
Adultery	*Two people, of whom at least one is married to someone else, having sexual relations*	*It is a sin against the committed bond of marriage. Couples are to work at strengthening their permanent commitment in marriage.*
Premarital sex	*Having sex before marriage*	*It is sexual activity without commitment and without the spiritual marriage bond that joins the couple for life.*
Artificial birth control	*Man-made devices, such as condoms, that prevent the conception and birth of a child*	*It tries to block artificially the purpose for which God intended human sexuality. The Church does not forbid natural methods of birth control, however.*

difference both to the individual and to the community—such as faithfulness, self-respect, and commitment.

 Name five ways that people your age can grow in appreciating God's gift of sexuality.

Love That Lasts

Sex is easy. Real love is hard work. Why? Real love requires discipline, self-control, and sensitivity. Real love requires generosity, thoughtfulness, and a high degree of unselfishness. Real lovers are devoted to the people they love; they are faithful, and they are happy. They are fun to be with, and you can trust them. People who really know how to love will genuinely care for you and will never hurt you. They are not afraid of sex, but they are smart enough not to mistake intense emotions and passionate feelings for love. They know that such feelings come and go but that love remains.

A problem in our time is that people presume that the only kind of love is sexual love and that the only good relationship is a sexual one. But friendship is love, too. There is no better, richer, more joyous, and more lasting love than friendship. Friendship is a much greater blessing than sex. Sex is part of the friendship of marriage, but sex without friendship is empty.

This is an important time in your life to be learning more about friendship. Friendship is much more fascinating than sex, and it is much more important for your future happiness. A good friendship is one of the most precious gifts of life. Friendship teaches us about love because it helps us overcome self-centeredness and shows us the joy that we can find in seeking the happiness of someone else.

This is what should be happening when people start to date. Dating ought to allow people who claim to care for each other to get to know each other better. People who are truly in love are not only attracted to each other; they have also discovered common values and ideals, similar interests and beliefs, and all kinds of things that they enjoy doing together. Dating should be a time for learning about and growing in friendship.

People can have sex but know very little about each other. Such people have not learned the difference between love and lust. *Lust* is an excessive, and often uncontrollable sexual desire that occurs in people who have not developed their sexuality in a healthy and responsible way. Lustful people are so enslaved by their sexual desires that they do not care whom they use or ruin to satisfy their needs.

Why Wait?

Many people think it does not matter too much if you do not wait until marriage to have sex with someone you love. You want sex, so you have it. That seems to be the trend of our times. Much in popular culture encourages us to deny ourselves nothing. We have needs, and we satisfy them. If there is something we want, we get it.

Do you think there is something wrong with this thinking? Why or why not?

All of us are affected by this thinking. This is why words such as *purity*, *modesty*, and *abstinence* sound so old-fashioned to us, like relics from a distant time. Purity helps us to have God's view of ourselves. It helps us to have a true love of others, as Jesus taught. It also helps us to look at the human body as truly a "temple of the holy Spirit" (1 Corinthians 6:19). This view of life requires the strength and self-control to choose not to engage in sexual activity until the right time. This is what we mean by abstinence.

Both purity and abstinence are protected and aided by modesty. *Modesty* is the virtue by which we express respect for ourselves and others by the way we dress, speak, and act.

These ideas are based on the fact that we are too precious and have too much dignity to give ourselves to someone carelessly or thoughtlessly. Love, especially sexual love, is something beautiful and honorable, and it should be used responsibly.

A Virtue for the Strong

Chastity is the virtue that calls us to use our sexuality in a reasonable, responsible, and faithful manner. Chaste sexual behavior harms neither ourselves nor others. The opposite of lust, chastity does not repress or deny our sexuality. Rather, chastity directs it to the service of real and faithful love.

Every person, whether married or single, is called to live a chaste life. Like any virtue, chastity must be developed and practiced. Because our sexual attractions and feelings are so strong, often overpowering, chastity requires discipline, self-denial, self-respect, and prayer. Chastity can be hard to learn. Chastity is a virtue, not of the timid and the weak, but of the wise and the strong.

Besides those already mentioned, sins against chastity also include masturbation, promiscuity, and prostitution.

Masturbation, also called self-abuse, is the act of deliberately stimulating one's sexual organs by oneself. The Church teaches that masturbation is a grave and serious matter because it denies the purpose of human sexual activity, which is the possibility of new life. Many people may worry about this question, especially during adolescence. The Church reminds us to pray and to seek wise advice in this matter.

Promiscuity describes a casual and superficial approach to sexual love. A promiscuous person is someone who has sex with a number of partners without regard to faithful commitment.

Prostitution is the buying and selling of sex, usually between strangers. Prostitution is wrong because the prostitute sells his or her body for money.

Homosexuality

Homosexuality is the condition in which a person is sexually attracted to someone of the same sex. The Church teaches that homosexual acts are contrary to the natural law and the purpose of sexuality as God created it. This is because such sexual acts can never result in the birth of children, the gift of life. Although the Church teaches that homosexual acts are sinful, it also teaches that homosexual persons should be treated with respect, and compassion. This is because homosexual persons do not choose their condition. Cruelty and discrimination against homosexual persons are morally wrong. All human beings are made in the image of God, no matter what their sexual orientation.

What an amazing gift and power God has given us in our sexuality. Jesus knew the power of this gift too, since he shared fully in our human nature. That is why we can always bring our wonder and worry about sexuality to him. He understands.

Teens experience a lot of pressure from their peers to become sexually active. Have you felt this pressure? How have you responded to it?

What do you think is the difference between sex and friendship?

My Thoughts…

In this chapter we have talked about the importance of good friendships. Many parishes have teen clubs or youth organizations. These are good places to make friends. If your parish has such a club or organization, why not join and discover what a good way it is to begin friendships?

YOU ARE MY WITNESSES

Scripture My Life

Perhaps you have heard this argument for premarital sex: "What's the big deal? Sex is the same whether we're married or not."

Evidently this is an idea that has a long history. The Book of Genesis in the Bible, however, describes married love this way: "A man leaves his father and mother and clings to his wife, and the two of them become one body" (Genesis 2:24). This isn't a description about the physical act; it is telling us that sexual love leads to a spiritual bond, a union of body *and* spirit.

CATHOLIC TEACHINGS

About Pornography

Pornography is the portrayal in words, movies, or pictures of sex or sexual activity in an obscene and degrading manner. Pornography takes what is meant to be a very personal and private expression of love and uses it to give unhealthy pleasure or satisfaction to others. Sexuality is beautiful; pornography is not. Pornography cheapens sexuality. It harms the dignity of both those who participate in it and those who take pleasure from it. It is especially evil when children are exploited by it.

CHAPTER 10

Called to Justice

Let justice surge like water,
and goodness like an unfailing stream.

Amos 5:24

An African folktale:

Animal (one that has no other name) came to the water hole to drink. He drank his fill and was leaving when Zebra came to drink. "Zebra will take all my water," Animal said. So he stayed and drank some more. The same thing happened when Giraffe and Gnu and Lion and Monkey came to drink. Animal drank all night long. He drank so much he drowned. What do you think is the moral of this story?

A Matter of Life or Death

If life has been good to you, perhaps you have never experienced real injustice. Maybe you have never gone to bed hungry, have always been able to get warm when you were cold, and have always had a nice home to return to each day. If so, you are one of the lucky ones.

Many of our sisters and brothers have not been so lucky. They go to bed hungry; they wander the streets; they feel overlooked and forgotten.

It is not supposed to be this way. When God created human beings, he meant for us to live together in justice and love. We were to share the goods of the earth, not hoard them. We were to care for our brothers and sisters. Wealth was not meant for only a few.

God's plan has not changed. People in some parts of our country are not supposed to starve while people in other parts have plenty. Men and women are not intended to lose their jobs because greedy corporate leaders and anxious stockholders want higher profits no matter what the consequences to other human beings. And the resources of the natural world are not to be torn apart just so a few can live in luxury. How do you think God feels about what we are doing with the gift of our world, a gift we received from him?

Called to Justice

Justice is emphasized throughout the Bible, especially in the Old Testament. The prophets constantly called the Israelites to be a people of justice because Israel's God was a God of justice.

Working for justice and being people of justice are not simply choices for the Catholic moral life; they are absolute requirements. If we are not just, we are not followers of Christ. In his very first sermon in the synagogue at Nazareth, Jesus said that God had appointed him "to bring glad tidings to the poor," "to proclaim liberty to captives," and "to let the oppressed go free" (Luke 4:18). If we are to be his disciples, our lives, too, must bring good news to the poor and freedom to all who are oppressed. If we wish to belong to the kingdom of God, we must work for justice now.

What exactly is justice? *Justice* is the virtue that guides our relations with all people. Justice makes sure that we respect the dignity of all human beings and honor their rights. Our faith reminds us that we are a human family. The virtue of justice demands that we seek the common good for this family. This means that we are called to share with others.

What does it mean to be just? Just people are fair; they keep their promises; they are mindful of others. They tell the truth, never cheat, and never take what does not belong to them. They are respectful and responsible. They are not careless with other people's property or with the good things of the earth. They know their obligations to others, and they fulfill those obligations.

The basic rule of justice is to bring only good to others and to heed all the responsibilities we have toward them. Justice is people watching out and caring for one another. True justice is the opposite of selfishness. Just people see one another as brothers and sisters in the Lord. They know that justice obliges them to balance their wants and needs against those of others. They realize that justice even demands that they sacrifice their own interests at times for the needs of their neighbors.

If we want to live a moral life, we must be people of justice. If we want to be faithful to God and true followers of Christ, we must be people of justice. If we are people of justice, we will find ourselves blessed. Then we will live by the words of the prophet Micah, who told what the Lord requires: "Only to do the right and to love goodness, and to walk humbly with your God" (Micah 6:8).

A Matter of Dignity

We become just people when we recognize, respect, and respond to the value and dignity of others as human beings. Why do racism and ethnic bias continue to be problems in our society and throughout the world? It is because one racial or ethnic group decides that another group is less than human, has no dignity or value, and therefore is not entitled to any rights.

Why do men and women continue to fight against the sin of sexism and struggle for equal rights and respect? Isn't it because many people wrongly persist in denying the equal dignity of both women and men? And why is it that so

many people believe it is all right to be cruel to men and women just because they have a homosexual orientation? And what about the rights of the elderly or the disabled? Why are people sometimes tempted to push them aside? Isn't it because they forget that all people are made in the image and likeness of God?

Justice depends on affirming the value of every person. The justice that God desires constantly reminds us that all people matter. What the world desperately needs is people strong and courageous enough to be just. What about you?

Can you think of some situations in our country and our world where justice is not at work?

A Command to Be Just

How would you feel if someone took an assignment you had worked hard on, then copied it, turned it in as his or her own work, and received the same grade as you? If you had any sense, you would be angry because someone had just taken from you what was rightfully yours.

The seventh commandment is "You shall not steal" (Exodus 20:15). To steal is to take what rightly belongs to another, whether it is money, goods from a department store, another person's work, or even natural resources. We steal when we shoplift, when we fail to pay back money we have borrowed, when we copy material from books and encyclopedias and present it as our own (this is called "plagiarism"), and when we copy from another person's test or homework and present it as our own work.

Citizens steal from their country when they cheat on their income tax forms. Employers steal when they do not pay just wages, when they break contracts they have made, and when they charge excessive prices for their goods. And rich countries steal from poor ones when they exploit them for their natural resources. Whether it is an individual, a business, or a nation that does it, taking what rightly belongs to another without permission or without just payment is stealing, and anyone who steals is a thief.

It is strange but true that many people do not believe stealing is wrong as long as they can get away with it. They do not seem to think twice about taking your money—as long as they do not get caught. Stealing does not bother their consciences. They are comfortable being thieves. They do not even admit that what they are doing is morally wrong.

The Church clearly tells us that our faith must be practiced in every part of our lives.

Why do so many people think that stealing is not wrong?

Discuss the injustices represented in these photographs.

82

Justice for All

Strange as it may sound, individuals, groups, and nations are also stealing when they own more than they justly should, especially at the expense of the poor. It may be legal to own so much, but it may not be moral. The rich steal from the poor when their excessive wealth prevents poor people from having even the most basic necessities of life, such as housing, food, clothing, and education. The Church teaches us in the name of Christ that God intended the goods of creation for the whole human race. Greed, materialism, and consumerism are sins against justice.

Catholic moral teaching has always supported the right to private property. But it has also insisted that this right be used to further the common good. All people have a right to property and enough money to make a decent life possible for themselves and their families. Having property and other possessions is not a bad thing. But that right is limited. It must in justice be balanced against the rights and needs of others, especially the poor. This is what we mean by the common good.

Give some examples of materialism and consumerism. Why are they sins against justice?

People or Profits?

Right now you are preparing to enter the workforce of the future. What do you think about work? What does your faith tell you about work?

The Church teaches us that everyone has the right to work. Work is not only essential for survival; it is also important for a person's sense of self-worth and dignity. All people need the opportunity to develop their talents through work and to feel that they can make a contribution to society. This is

The Dignity of Work

Human work has had a special dignity from the very beginning. In the Old Testament God himself is pictured as a worker, a marvelous craftsman. In the New Testament Joseph, the foster father of Jesus, was a carpenter. We have no doubt that Jesus worked; he was probably a carpenter, too.

Workers have responsibilities. A worker must work honestly and responsibly and give a fair day's work for fair pay. Moreover it is wrong to make money from activities that are immoral. This is why it is absolutely wrong, for example, to make a living by selling drugs, producing pornography, or supporting or being involved in prostitution.

The Needs of the Poor

Both individuals and society have a moral obligation to respond to the needs of the poor, especially those who are unable to find work or to support themselves.

As Catholics we have a special obligation to be attentive to the needs of the poor. Read the story of the rich man and Lazarus (Luke 16:19–31) to find out how Jesus felt about the poor. As individuals and nations we have a responsibility to love the poor and help them. They are our brothers and sisters, and Christ lives in them. What we do for anyone in need, Jesus tells us, we do for him.

 Take a minute to read Matthew 25:31–46. What does Jesus say about those who care for the poor?

why no one should be discriminated against in employment. People have a right to apply for any positions for which they may be qualified.

In recent years hundreds of thousands of American workers have lost their jobs simply because employers figured that the best way to increase profits is to reduce the number of employees. To think that profits are more important than people is morally wrong. Although the Church teaches that companies have a right to make a profit, it also stresses that people are more important than profits.

Here is the basic teaching of the Church on justice in the workplace:

The Good of Persons

Those in charge of corporations and businesses have a moral obligation to consider the good of persons as well as the increase of profits. They must provide a safe and secure environment for their workers.

A Just Wage

Employers are obliged to give their workers a just wage. A just wage means fair pay for the work being done. Workers are entitled to what they need in order to provide a good life for themselves and their families.

CATHOLIC ID A disciple of Jesus is someone who rejoices in the good fortune of others. The opposite is someone who feels envy. We envy others when we are jealous of what they have and would take it for ourselves if we could. Sometimes envious people go so far as to wish harm on those they envy. We are obliged by the tenth commandment not to covet our neighbor's goods (Exodus 20:17).

Do you think that destroying or defacing private or public property is a kind of stealing? Why or why not?

The Church teaches that our right to property and possessions must be balanced against the needs of others. Explain that teaching.

My Thoughts…

Many parishes have committees or other organizations, such as the Saint Vincent de Paul Society, that focus on justice and service to the poor. Before Christmas or during Lent, many parishes collect food or clothing for the poor. Get involved with one of these organizations or projects. See what it teaches you about justice and our duty as followers of Christ to care for those in need.

YOU ARE MY WITNESSES

Scripture My Life

Scripture is filled with references to a life of justice. We need only think of the prophets, the gospels, and the letters of the New Testament. Here are a few words of advice that sound very modern:

Tell the rich in the present age not to be proud and not to rely on so uncertain a thing as wealth but rather on God, who richly provides us with all things for our enjoyment. Tell them to do good, to be rich in good works, to be generous, ready to share, thus accumulating as treasure a good foundation for the future.

1 Timothy 6:17–19

Catholic Teachings

About Restitution

Restitution is the return of or payment for something stolen from another. Restitution is a moral obligation of justice; it is a way of repairing whatever damage or loss another person or group has suffered on account of one's crime. Sometimes it is impossible to return exactly what has been taken. In such cases something of the same value must be substituted. If we have stolen something, it is not enough just to be sorry. We must in justice pay back what we have taken.

Called to Truth

Jesus, you are the way,
the truth, and the life.

> *"Rather than love, than money, than fame, give me truth."*
> Henry David Thoreau

Is truth that important?
What do you think it means to tell and live by the truth?

Built on Trust

What do we mean by the truth? The truth is something that really exists. It means that something is a fact. Truth is something that we can trust, something or someone that we believe. For example, we know that the sun gives light and heat. We trust in this fact every day of our lives because we know it is true.

To know the truth is very important for human beings. Yet seeking and telling the truth don't always seem to be popular. Some people approve of lying if they can get away with it. Sometimes people say, "If lying makes your life easier, why not do it?" or "If lying helps you to get ahead or make more money, why not do it?"

What would the world be like if no one cared about the truth? We certainly could not live in community and trust one another. The only way people can live together is by telling the truth. A community or a family can only exist and be happy when it is built on trust, truth, and honesty.

What would you say to someone who tells you that little white lies make no difference in life?

The Source of All Truth

Living by the truth means much more than not telling lies. We know from our faith and the teachings of the Church that there is only one source of all truth. And that source is the living God. God is the source and perfection of all truth.

God alone is worthy of our absolute and complete trust. God never lies. This is why we can say that God's law is true, his word is true, and all his ways are true.

As Christians we know that the fullness of God's truth has been revealed to us in Jesus Christ. He is the Word of God made flesh among us. He is "full of grace and truth" (John 1:14). Jesus said that he is "the way and the truth and the life" (John 14:6). As followers of Christ we turn away from evil and from the devil, who is called "the father of lies" (John 8:44).

In this chapter we shall explore the ways that living by the truth helps us to become truly human, as God intended.

A Moral Obligation

Have you ever been around people who lie all the time? After lying so often, they can no longer tell the difference between a lie and the truth. They have taken the gift of speech, which is given by God, and used it in a way that is exactly the opposite of what God intends.

Truth is so important for us that Jesus promised to send us the Holy Spirit, the Spirit of truth. The Holy Spirit, Jesus said, will "guide you to all truth" (John 16:13). Truth is essential to our lives as Catholics. If we are not truthful in our dealings with people, we deny them what is rightfully theirs in justice. Lying is like stealing; it deprives people lied to of the truth that they have every right to know. So when we tell the truth, we are not simply being nice or thoughtful or considerate. Rather, we are being just because the truth is something that is due every human being.

The eighth commandment forbids lying and commands that we speak the truth: "You shall not bear false witness against your neighbor" (Exodus 20:16). In forbidding us to lie to or deceive other people, it commands us to be truthful and honest with them. It does so not only because our life together depends on it but also because, as our neighbors, others have a right to the truth.

The most common way we sin against the eighth commandment is by lying. *Lying* is speaking or acting untruthfully in a way that deceives someone who has the right to know the truth.

We can also lie with our actions when we knowingly suggest by our behavior something that is not actually the case. The common name for this deceptive and misleading behavior is *hypocrisy*. A hypocrite is someone who puts on a false appearance. Hypocrites are liars.

CATHOLIC ID Catholics honor the saints who gave their lives for the sake of the truth. We call these saints *martyrs*. Martyrs are men and women who, by giving up their lives, witness to the truth of the gospel and to Christ our Savior. The stories of the martyrs tell of courageous people who overcame fear and were able to endure anything for the truth. Choose a martyr of faith, and ask him or her to pray that you will be a strong witness to Christ, too.

Gossip: Is It Harmless?

The story is told of a gossipy person who asked one of the saints for God's forgiveness. The saint told the person that reparation must be made for the sin of gossip and for ruining another's reputation. The saint said, "Go to the top of a high hill. Take a feather pillow, and let all the feathers fly into the wind. Then go and pick up all the feathers." The person said, "But that's impossible to do!" The saint replied, "So, too, is it impossible to repair the damage done to another by hurtful gossip."

Many people love to gossip and pass on rumors about others. Gossip sells because we like to hear tidbits about other people's lives, especially if the tidbits are slightly embarrassing. Is there anything wrong with this?

Yes. Gossip is like a weed. It can grow anywhere. Like an uncontrollable wildfire it spreads in neighborhoods, especially when somebody new and perhaps a little different moves in. And gossip certainly finds a home at school. Students love to gossip. Everybody knows who has the latest rumor about somebody else.

Gossip is usually harmful. Many people have had their reputations ruined because of false or nasty rumors. Many people have suffered terribly because of lies that have been whispered behind their backs. And this happens at all ages and at all levels of life.

Why do people gossip? Gossip gives them a sense of power. Part of that power is knowing that what they say can seriously hurt others. The trouble with gossip is that it cannot be controlled. When people start a rumor, they think that they can decide who will hear it and where it will go after it leaves their lips. But they cannot. Someone may start a rumor with the intention of doing nothing more than getting a little revenge. But by the time it has done its work, another person's reputation may be ruined.

The Church teaches that spreading lies about people and causing others to judge them falsely and harshly is to commit the sin of *calumny*. A slightly different kind of sin is detraction. People commit the sin of *detraction* when they speak of someone's faults and failings to others without good reason, even if those faults and failings are true. The sin of detraction, like the sin of calumny, is most often committed for the purpose of harming a person's good name. There are other sins against the eighth commandment, too. One of them is *rash judgment*. To judge someone rashly is to assume something about the person without any evidence.

Finally self-deception is also an offense against the truth. *Self-deception* is lying to oneself about one's abilities or behavior, usually because one is unable or unwilling to see the truth about oneself. This is an especially dangerous form of lying because it is hard to detect and deal with and also because it can cause great harm to oneself and others.

Did you think there could be so much involved in being a truthful person? What challenges to the truth do you meet in your everyday life?

Truthful Disciples

Jesus tells us why the truth is so necessary in our lives. He says, "If you remain in my word, you will truly be my disciples, and you will know the truth, and the truth will set you free" (John 8:31–32). We will only be free if we try each day to live truthfully. This means that we must look at the world and at others with the eyes of Christ.

It is not easy to be strong witnesses to the truth. Even Jesus' closest disciples were afraid of the truth at times. Do you remember the story of Jesus' arrest? After he was arrested, the disciples ran away. They could not face what was about to happen to Jesus. Only when they were strengthened by the power of the risen Christ and the coming of the Holy Spirit were they able to be strong witnesses.

The eighth commandment calls us to be truthful in our speech and in our actions. But we cannot be truthful in our actions unless we have a truthful vision of life. A good action begins in a truthful vision. Without that vision we cannot act rightly. For instance, a person who looks at everything through eyes of anger and bitterness is a miserable person to be around. And someone whose vision of life is twisted by violence will probably be cruel and harsh, too.

Every act of cruelty or injustice really comes from a person's refusal to see the truth about another human being. Each of us is created by God and possesses a unique dignity. If we do not see this, we cannot be just and truthful in our actions.

Can you think of an example in history, past or contemporary, of a lack of vision that resulted in evil?

Shaping Our Vision

What are some of the things that shape our vision of life? Our families certainly do; so do our friends. We are also shaped by the world we live in; our own experiences; our religious beliefs and convictions; and our teachers and leaders.

At this time in your life, one of the most powerful influences on the way you see life comes from your peers. In a sense you shape one another. You shape one another's values, attitudes, and feelings about other people and about life. This "peer pressure" can be quite positive, especially if you are blessed with good friends. But peer pressure can also be harmful if your peers encourage attitudes that lead to discrimination, cruelty, or meanness. What kinds of attitudes and behavior do your peers urge you to adopt? Are they shaping in you a vision that is truthful and good or one that is false and unhealthy?

When all is said and done, the truth always works better than a lie. Truth sets us free. That's why Jesus told us: "If you remain in my word, you will truly be my disciples, and you will know the truth, and the truth will set you free" (John 8:31–32).

All lies are wrong, but some lies are more serious than others. For example, covering up your laziness by telling a teacher that the dog ate your homework is certainly a lie and wrong. However, it is not nearly as wrong as lying about another person in order to ruin his or her reputation. Can you see why the second example is a more seriously sinful lie than the first?

Lying is a form of stealing from someone who has a right to the truth. Therefore we must make an act of reparation to the person to whom we have lied, just as we must perform an act of restitution if we have stolen something. An act of *reparation* tries to repair or make up for the damage done by a lie.

We make reparation by admitting to the lie and telling the truth. If we have harmed a person's reputation by gossip and lies, we have a moral obligation to undo that behavior. First we admit to the lie both to that person and to all others with whom we have spoken about it. Then we must do all we can to restore the person's good name by speaking the truth about him or her.

Can you think of a time when gossip about a fellow student or a friend hurt that person and was unfair to him or her? How did people deal with this?

How do movies and music shape your attitudes? How would you describe the "vision of life" behind the music you like or the movies you see?

My Thoughts…

OnLine WITH THE PARISH

Parish churches often have statues, stained glass, or even small shrines honoring saints special to that parish. Read an account of the life of a saint honored in your parish. Then think about the way that saint was a witness to Christ and the gospel in his or her life. How could you be a better witness to Christ in your own life?

YOU ARE MY WITNESSES

Scripture My Life

Jesus warned us about the dangers of rash judgment and encouraged in us a more compassionate and truthful vision of others. He said, "Why do you notice the splinter in your brother's eye, but do not perceive the wooden beam in your own eye?" (Matthew 7:3)

What does this tell you about the dangers of judging others and about hypocrisy?

Catholic Teachings

About Truth

The Church teaches that everyone has a right to the truth. However, we must respect everyone's right to privacy and never tell what has been given to us in confidence unless a very serious reason demands it. For example, we should never keep a confidence about a serious matter such as the selling of drugs or the suicidal feelings of a friend.

The most sacred obligation to silence and secrecy is that of the sacrament of Reconciliation. The *seal of confession* is the solemn obligation of a priest never to tell what has been told to him in this sacrament.

Virtues: Skills for Life's Journey

*Show me the path I should walk,
for to you I entrust my life.*

Psalm 143:8

The Christian moral life really demands a great deal. Is God asking too much of us? Isn't it really impossible to be so good?

Living Powerful Lives

Many people seem to be able to live a deeply moral life. Where do they get the power and strength to do this?

The following stories are about people who have done powerful things in difficult situations. They are about people of virtue. *Virtue* is a word that means "power." After you read the stories, see whether you can describe in one or two words the power, or virtue, being practiced by these people.

• Some young friends make their way down the street, talking and laughing. They are spread across the sidewalk in such a way that no one can possibly get through them. Suddenly, from around the corner, an elderly woman carrying groceries appears. One of the group sees her and says, "Hey, guys, let's move over and let this lady through."

The virtue, or power, shown here is _____

_____

• A family that lives down the street from you has a young child named Billy, who has Down's syndrome. When Billy was born, many people thought that he should be sent to an institution. It would be too difficult and too sad, they thought, for the family to care for him. But the family chose to keep Billy with them. They work as a team to make sure that his life is as full as possible. Whenever you see members of this family, they always look happy, especially when Billy is around.

The virtue, or power, shown here is _____

_____

Habits That Heal

The people you have just read about are powerful people. They do not wait for the "big" moment to come along. Instead they choose to live a good life, a virtuous life, in daily situations. It is in these same types of situations that we, too, begin to practice what it means to be a virtuous person. This is where our Catholic morality becomes very practical. It deals with the way our daily lives are supposed to be lived. Our everyday choices determine the direction our lives will take. What will you make of yourself? What kind of person will you be five or ten years from now?

These are questions you should be asking now because your future is being shaped in part by the choices you make today. Every time you act, you say something about the person you want to be tomorrow. It is a matter of choice. Your future grows out of the choices you make today.

Virtues empower us to make good choices. We need virtues because even though we are called to grow in goodness, holiness, and love, we can give in to temptations. We can use our freedom to sin.

We can make choices that turn us away from what is good and right.

Our human nature is weakened and wounded by sin, especially the lingering effects of original sin. There is a way for us to heal those wounds and to grow stronger in goodness. Along with God's grace and the help that comes to us through the sacraments, the virtues weaken the hold sin has on our lives. Virtues help us overcome temptations and strengthen us in doing what is right. In other words, just as sin makes us "morally sick," virtues make us "morally healthy."

What exactly is a virtue? Catholics define a *virtue* as a good habit that empowers a person to act according to reason and faith. This means that in order to act in a virtuous way, we must use our minds and be guided by our faith. A virtue makes acting in a certain way easy, even spontaneous. It helps us not only to do what is right but also to give the best of ourselves joyfully. In fact the Church teaches that "the goal of a virtuous life is to become like God" (*Catechism,* 1803).

There are several important things we must know about virtues. They are that virtues are qualities of character, are skills, and take practice.

Virtues Are Qualities of Character We must *decide* to be virtuous people. Virtues represent what we have made of ourselves through our most characteristic behavior. For example, we would call people courteous because they habitually treat others with respect. Being courteous has become part of who they are and what they do.

Actual photograph of Saint Thérèse of Lisieux, age 13

CATHOLIC ID

A person who practices virtue is *virtuous*. A person who practices vice is *vicious*. Have you ever thought of this? Virtuous or vicious—each takes practice. Followers of Jesus, especially the saints, know this. That is why Catholics cherish the writings of the saints, in which they very often tell us about living a virtuous life.

Virtues Are Skills   A virtuous person has the wisdom and skill to know how to do good in whatever way it needs to be done. When we speak of the virtues as habits, we do not mean that a virtuous person is someone who does the same thing in exactly the same way all the time. Rather, the virtuous person has the imagination and insight needed to do what is good in the best way possible, no matter what the situation or circumstances may be.

Virtues Take Practice   We can develop virtues, but this takes effort and practice. If we are to become truly virtuous people, we must work at it and develop patterns of good actions in our lives.

The opposite of virtues are *vices*. Like the virtues, vices are habitual and characteristic ways of acting. Unlike virtues, however, vices are evil acts that, if done repeatedly, will weaken and deform a person's character. It is always up to us. When we choose the way of virtue, we give the best of ourselves.

Do you consistently use bad language? Practice changing your language for a week. Eventually good language will become a power in your life—a virtue.

The Cardinal Virtues

Imagine your life as a journey. What is needed for a good and successful life's journey? The Church teaches that anyone who hopes to make his or her way successfully through all of life must have four key virtues. These are called the cardinal virtues. The word *cardinal* comes from a word meaning "hinge." All the other human virtues depend, or are hinged, on the four cardinal virtues: prudence, justice, temperance, and fortitude.

The first cardinal virtue is prudence. *Prudence* is really common sense. It is practical wisdom or right judgment about what needs to be done in any given situation or circumstance. Prudence is the first of the cardinal virtues because it helps us see how we ought to act before we act. Prudent people have enough sense to avoid behavior that might harm themselves or others. For example:

- Prudent drivers do not drive recklessly.
- Prudent people never go out on a boat without life jackets.

Every other virtue depends on prudence. For instance, we could not be just or fair without prudence. We would not know exactly how to give each of the different people in our lives what he or she deserves. We could not be truly courageous without prudence. This is because prudence helps us to see the difference between real bravery and recklessness.

Prudence is *knowing* what needs to be done; justice is *doing* what needs to be done. The second cardinal virtue is justice. *Justice* is right action. People who are just give what is due to their neighbors and to God. Without justice there can be no peace, no common good.

The third cardinal virtue is temperance. *Temperance* helps us control and direct our emotions. Instead of being overpowered by emotions and possibly doing wrong because of them, temperance helps us to use them to do what is good. For example:

- A temperate person, when angry, does not scream or try to hurt someone.
- A temperate person does not eat or drink to excess.
- A temperate person also knows when too much dieting or too much exercise can be unhealthy.

Temperate people live in the real world, not only in their imaginations. They live a balanced life that expresses their dignity as human beings.

The fourth cardinal virtue is fortitude. *Fortitude*, or courage, helps us when we are tempted to turn from what is right because of fear or discouragement. It strengthens us to resist temptations and not to give up when we face difficulties in living morally.

Write in the chart an explanation of each virtue and an example of the way each virtue can help you live a good life.

Cardinal Virtue	Meaning	Example
Prudence		
Justice		
Temperance		
Fortitude		

The Way to God

The virtues are the skills that we need to reach our goals and fulfill the purposes of our lives on earth. But what if our goal is heaven? And what if God invites us to share in his very own life?

He has. Through grace. That is why even the cardinal virtues will not be enough for us to reach our heavenly goal. The cardinal virtues equip us to deal with the challenges and opportunities of this world, but they are not all we need to live the life of grace. To participate in the divine life is far beyond our human powers. The cardinal virtues are *human* powers, powers that we acquire ourselves, with God's help. To reach God, however, we need *divine* powers, powers that come from God alone. These divine powers are called the *theological* virtues.

There are three theological virtues: faith, hope, and love. We cannot give ourselves these virtues because they are beyond our human reach. Rather, each is a gift from God that enables us to live for God and with God in order to become like God. The theological virtues make it possible for us to share God's life right now. Their goal is to make us friends of God in this world so that we can enjoy perfect happiness with him in heaven. Like any virtue, each is meant to change us. The theological virtues change us by making us like God. If we live them fully, we become saints.

Faith   Through the theological virtue of faith, we believe in God and all that he has said and revealed to us and all that the Catholic Church teaches us. We have faith in God because we believe that he is truth itself. Faith reminds us that human beings are fulfilled, not through understanding human truths alone, but through knowing and believing in the supernatural truths found in God. Through the gift of faith, we entrust ourselves completely to God. In doing so, we come to know God as

the source of all life, goodness, and truth and as the one in whom we find joy and salvation.

Faith is a gift that we must care for and protect. We do so by accepting and living the truths of faith; by participating in the sacraments, especially the Eucharist; and by living a life of prayer.

Can the gift of faith be weakened in us? Yes. Faith is weakened when we harden our minds and hearts to God, when we stubbornly refuse to believe, and when we are neglectful and careless with this gift.

Hope   Through the theological virtue of hope, we desire eternal life as our ultimate happiness. We trust in the promises of Christ, whose resurrection gives us the confident hope that death will be overcome by life, that goodness will conquer evil, and that we will be saved and blessed with the fullness of life.

People of hope never stop believing in all of life's possibilities, no matter what. They remember always, even in periods of hardship and suffering, that God loves them and wants what is best for them. During times of discouragement they never surrender or give in to defeat. Rather, they continue to aspire to what is best, especially the goodness and glory of God.

Love   Through the virtue of love, we love God above everything else, for his own sake. And we love our neighbor as ourselves for the love of

God. Love makes our life a friendship with God and an imitation of Christ. Through this virtue we not only love but love as God loves. As we read in the New Testament, "Beloved, let us love one another, because love is of God; everyone who loves is begotten by God and knows God" (1 John 4:7).

Which of the cardinal virtues do you think is most difficult for people your age to practice? Explain.

What symbols would you use to help describe faith, hope, and love? Sketch your ideas.

My Thoughts…

There are many good people in our parishes, people who inspire us by their dedication, kindness, generosity, and prayerfulness. They are virtuous people, unsung heroes who make the world better. What can you learn from them? What do they teach you about goodness and the virtuous life?

YOU ARE MY WITNESSES

Scripture My Life

Saint Paul wrote about a life lived in the Spirit (Galatians 5:16–26). Life in the Spirit is marked by love, joy, peace, patience, kindness, generosity, faithfulness, gentleness, and self-control. These qualities are sometimes called the "fruits of the Spirit" because they describe people who are living for the kingdom of God, as Jesus taught us.

Catholic Teachings

About the Gifts of the Spirit
The Holy Spirit comes to us with gifts that help in our efforts to live a virtuous life. These are the seven gifts of the Holy Spirit: wisdom, understanding, right judgment, courage, knowledge, reverence, and wonder and awe. The gifts of the Holy Spirit help us to live the fullness of the Christian moral life. Through these gifts a person becomes completely responsive to God, doing God's will in all things.

101

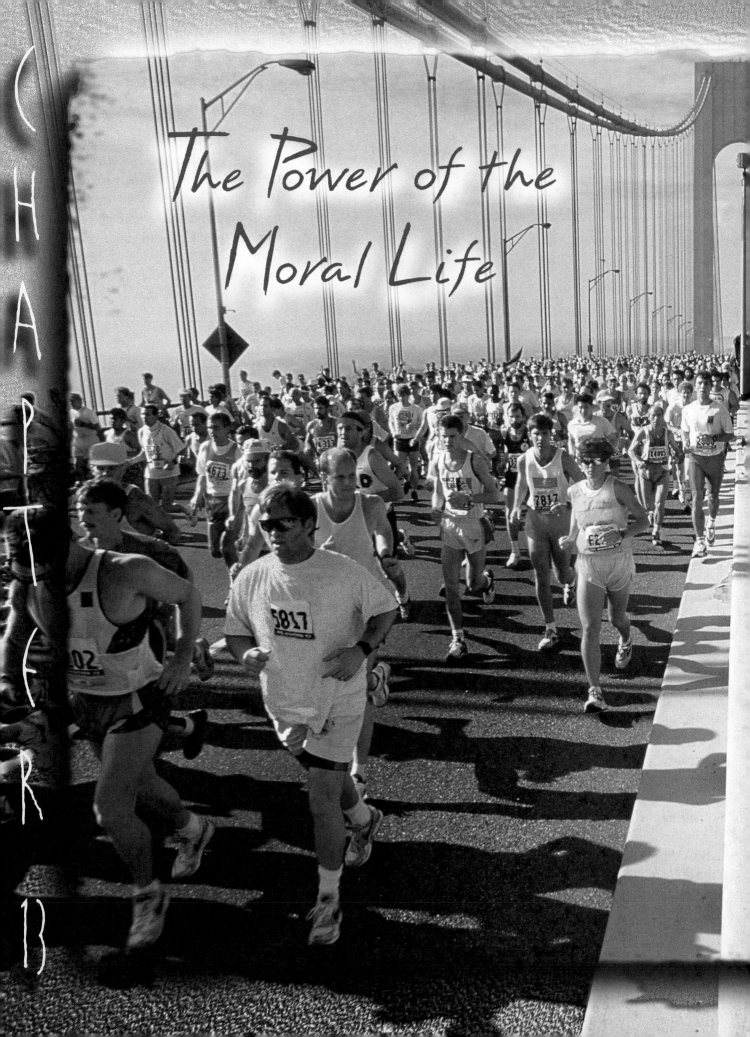

CHAPTER 13

The Power of the
Moral Life

Lord Jesus,
you are the strength of the weak
and the prize of the strong.
Book of Blessings

Saint Paul said that followers of Christ were to be like powerful athletes running a race, stretching for the finish line and the prize. Do you think that trying to live a good life is like running toward a goal?

Stretching Toward the Goal

Each of us needs a goal in life, something that urges us on to do the best and be the best possible. True athletes do this. They train and practice as hard as they can to achieve their best, to cross the finish line. They let no obstacle or excuse stand in their way or sidetrack them.

Saint Paul said that Christians have the greatest goal of all: We are to be like Jesus Christ. For the Christian each day is a day of training. Each day is an opportunity to practice being the best we can be. This is the way we reach our goal, which is Christ.

During this course we have looked at many of the "rules" that direct us to our goal and help us live as followers of Christ: the Beatitudes, the Ten Commandments, and the virtues. Like athletes we need these rules; once we learn them, they become part of us. Then we can live them and practice them naturally. This is what Jesus wants us to do. He challenges us every day to be the best disciples that we can be.

To give an example of what he meant, Jesus told the parable of the Good Samaritan (Luke 10:29–37): Once there was a man who was attacked on the road by robbers and left for dead. Two people from his own country came by and saw him. But they did nothing. For whatever reason each of them walked by and did not help. Then a foreigner, a Samaritan, came by. Without hesitating, he reached out to the wounded man and cared for him. The Samaritan even took him to an inn and paid for his lodging and further care. This foreigner did not have to take time to think about what was the right thing to do. He knew what was right. It was a part of him.

After telling the parable, Jesus asked his listeners which person in the story was living the way God wanted. The foreigner, the Samaritan, was the person who did not fail to act. This was the person truly living a moral life.

What a challenge Jesus puts before us! How exciting to be asked to live this Christian life, to have the goal of becoming like him! Are you ready to accept this challenge and to "persevere in running the race that lies before us while keeping our eyes fixed on Jesus" (Hebrews 12:1–2)?

What obstacles could hold a person back from accepting the challenge of Jesus to live the moral life? How could these challenges be overcome?

The Laws of the Church

We are called to high standards. We are to live the Beatitudes and to obey the Ten Commandments and are expected to practice the virtues. At the same time, however, the Church realizes our human tendency to get out of focus and take the easy way out. That is why the Church gives us certain laws that help us to fulfill our obligations as Catholics. These are called the laws, or the precepts, of the Church.

• *Celebrate Christ's resurrection every Sunday (or Saturday evening) and on holy days of*

obligation by taking part in the Mass and avoiding unnecessary work. The Eucharist is the center, the "source and summit," of our lives. All Catholics have the obligation to participate in the Mass on Sundays and holy days. Millions of Catholics frequently join in worshiping God at daily Mass as well.

• *Lead a sacramental life. Receive Holy Communion frequently and the sacrament of Penance, or Reconciliation, regularly.* We must receive Holy Communion at least once a year at Lent—Easter. We must confess within a year if we have committed serious, or mortal, sin. The Church is reminding us of the importance and beauty of the Eucharist and of sacramental confession. Catholics who are determined to strengthen their moral life will certainly go well beyond these minimum requirements.

• *Study Catholic teaching throughout life, especially in preparing for the sacraments.* Studying our faith throughout our life is essential to forming our identity as Catholics.

• *Observe the marriage laws of the Catholic Church and give religious training to one's children.* One of the laws governing the sacrament of Matrimony states that

How can celebrating the Eucharist together help you keep your focus?

Catholics who are free to marry must be married in the presence of a priest and two witnesses. In addition Catholic parents are seriously obliged to have their children baptized and to bring them up as practicing Catholics.

• *Strengthen and support the Church: one's own parish, the worldwide Church, and our Holy Father, the pope.* One obvious way of giving support is through the offering of money. But support also includes prayer and the giving of our time and talents, especially in our parish.

• *Do penance, including not eating meat and fasting from food on certain days.* Catholics in the United States who are fourteen years of age and older are obliged to abstain from eating meat on Ash Wednesday and all the Fridays of Lent unless reasons of health excuse them. Catholics between the ages of twenty-one and fifty-nine are obliged to fast—that is, limit themselves to one full meal and two smaller meals—on Ash Wednesday and Good Friday.

• *Join in the missionary work of the Church.* By Baptism we are called to be missionaries to those around us.

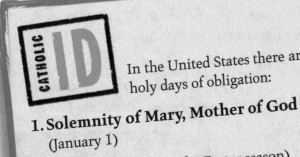

In the United States there are six holy days of obligation:

1. **Solemnity of Mary, Mother of God** (January 1)

2. **Ascension** (during the Easter season)

3. **Assumption of Mary** (August 15)

4. **All Saints' Day** (November 1)

5. **Immaculate Conception** (December 8)

6. **Christmas** (December 25)

The Works of Mercy

We Catholics are called to live our lives as followers of Jesus and members of the Church. This way of life includes what we call the Works of Mercy. *Mercy* means showing love and compassion to those who are suffering.

Jesus challenged his disciples to act mercifully and told them that whatever they did for one of the least of their brothers and sisters, they did for him (Matthew 25:40). What did Jesus mean? He was telling us that whenever we carry out a work of mercy, we are actually doing Christ's work in the world.

The risen Christ is now present in the world. As his followers we are to look for the face of Christ in every person we meet, especially in those who are suffering or in need. The Works of Mercy demand of us a spirit of loving service, as Jesus taught. He said, "I have given you a model to follow, so that as I have done for you, you should also do" (John 13:15).

Catholics divide the Works of Mercy into two groups. We call the one group "corporal" because these works of mercy are concerned with the material and physical needs of others. The other group we call "spiritual" because they deal with the needs of the heart and mind and soul. Perhaps there is no more practical way of testing our growth in the moral life than by seeing how we are carrying out the Works of Mercy in our lives.

Try to memorize the Works of Mercy listed in the chart. Then complete the chart with your own ideas.

Works of Mercy

Corporal	Example	Something I Can Do
Feed the hungry.	Working in a parish food pantry	
Give drink to the thirsty.	Building irrigation projects in mission lands	
Clothe the naked.	Working for the St. Vincent de Paul Society	
Help those imprisoned.	Ministering to prisoners, especially as chaplains or teachers	
Shelter the homeless.	Providing a home for a refugee family	
Care for the sick.	Doing volunteer work in a Catholic hospital	
Bury the dead.	Treating cemeteries with respect	

Spiritual		
Share our knowledge with others.	Knowing your faith well so that you can share it	
Give advice to those who need it.	Giving good example	
Comfort those who suffer.	Making yourself available to those in need	
Be patient with others.	Taking time to listen to others	
Forgive those who hurt us.	Being willing to let go of a grudge; not wanting to take revenge	
Give correction to those who need it.	Being honest with friends when they do wrong	
Pray for the living and the dead.	Participating in Mass on the anniversary of a relative's death	

A Balanced Approach

Sometimes we think that the good things we do in life are only between God and us. Not so. Our moral life connects us to everybody and everything. Our actions sometimes have consequences far beyond what we intend or even imagine.

Every time we act, someone or something is affected. If we perform even a simple act of kindness, someone is blessed. If we commit even a single act of thoughtlessness, someone is hurt. We cannot avoid the consequences of our actions, whether they are small or large. We are part of a community of life: Everything we do has consequences for others; and every time we act, something in the universe is affected.

Sometimes, however, people say, "We can do anything we want to reach our goals as long as the goals are good. We can use any means we have to get the end results we know are right." For example, a young person really wants to please a parent and decides to get good grades by cheating. The goal, or end result, of pleasing a parent may be a good one. But it should never be achieved by using dishonest means. The Church teaches that the end does not justify the means. In other words, in this case, the end (pleasing a parent) does not justify the means (cheating).

 Can you think of other examples in which the ends do not justify the means?

Power to Change the World

Perhaps you have realized by now that you are quite a remarkable person. You have the potential for great power within you, just by the way you live your everyday life. Everyday behavior has power to change lives. We can change lives through our kindness and our thoughtfulness, our compassion and friendliness, our joy and our love. Anyone who can help others this way is pretty powerful. And you can do this!

The most powerful moral act is the gift of kindness that one person gives to another. With every such act, grace gets "passed around," and God's life breaks a little more fully into our world.

Which law of the Church do you find most challenging? Tell why.

Why is it important to be aware that your actions have consequences for the world around you?

My Thoughts…

The names of couples planning to be married are printed in your parish bulletins. Check the most recent bulletin for these names. Even if you do not know these people, pray for them by name as they prepare for their wedding and married life.

YOU ARE MY WITNESSES

Scripture of My Life

Jesus taught that love is the greatest commandment (Luke 10:25–28). Those who claim to be followers of Jesus must be people of mercy and love. One of the New Testament writers gives a reason for this: "If anyone says, 'I love God,' but hates his brother, he is a liar; for whoever does not love a brother whom he has seen cannot love God whom he has not seen. This is the commandment we have from him: whoever loves God must also love his brother" (1 John 4:20–21).

Catholic Teachings

About Mary and the Moral Life

When faced with the struggles that are a part of living the moral life, Catholics often turn to the Blessed Virgin Mary. Pope John Paul II reminded us of Mary's importance in our lives. He wrote that Mary, the mother of mercy, is the "radiant sign and inviting model of the moral life" (*The Splendor of Truth*, 120). Take a moment to think about the hard choices Mary had to make in life. Ask her to help you make your hard choices.

CHAPTER 14

Making Moral Decisions

To do your will is my delight;
my God, your law is in my heart!

Psalm 40:9

I shall be telling this with a sigh
Somewhere ages and ages hence:
Two roads diverged in a wood, and I—
I chose the one less traveled by.
And that has made all the difference.

Robert Frost

Have you ever made a choice that made an important difference in your life?

All the Difference

We make decisions all the time, every day, often without even being conscious that we are doing it. We decide, for example, what to eat, what to wear, what to do after school, what to watch on TV. It goes on and on. Obviously many of these choices are simple and uncomplicated; they do not require a great deal of thought or energy. In fact we'd probably go crazy if we had to go through a special process each time we made choices like these.

There are other decisions, however, that demand much more from us. They require attention and reflection and prayer. Why? Because these decisions affect our lives

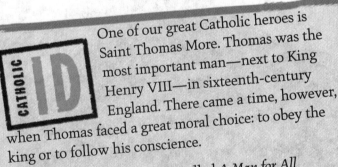

CATHOLIC ID

One of our great Catholic heroes is Saint Thomas More. Thomas was the most important man—next to King Henry VIII—in sixteenth-century England. There came a time, however, when Thomas faced a great moral choice: to obey the king or to follow his conscience.

In a twentieth-century play called *A Man for All Seasons*, More tells his daughter why he cannot go against his conscience even to save his life. More says, "When a man takes an oath, Meg, he's holding his own self in his own hands, like water. And if he opens his fingers *then*—he needn't hope to find himself again."

When you have to face a serious moral decision, remember Thomas More.

deeply and significantly. They are moral decisions to do what is right or what is wrong, what is good or what is evil. As Frost's poem suggests, decisions like these can make "all the difference."

During this course we have explored what it means to live a moral life. We have learned that to be moral means to be truly human, to be what God created us to be: human beings made in his image and likeness. To be moral means to turn away from sin and cooperate with God's grace. To be moral means to be transformed by Christ, to follow his example and the teachings of his Church.

This is indeed a challenge. And it sets up the most important moral questions each of us has to answer personally: What kind of person am I becoming? And what kind of person do I want to become? Think about this. Then list five characteristics that you think describe a truly human person.

A truly human person is:

☐ _____

☐ _____

☐ _____

☐ _____

☐ _____

Now put an X in the box beside any characteristic that you feel describes you. Ask yourself: How will I go about developing the other qualities?

Check the Influences

The first thing we need to examine whenever we are faced with a moral decision is the influences at work. Take a look at some of the important influences in your life before reading the case study.

113

Influences in Decision Making	
❑ **common sense**	*What is my brain telling me? Does this make sense? What are the possible consequences?*
❑ **parents/family**	*What do my parents expect of me? What have they taught me?*
❑ **friends**	*What will my friends think? Is there any peer pressure at work?*
❑ **conscience**	*What do I know to be right or wrong?*
❑ **personal values**	*What is really important to me, not just at this moment, but in the long term? What kind of a person do I want to be?*

A Case Study

Lauren's parents were going away over the weekend, leaving her older sister in charge. Lauren thought it would be fun to have six friends stay overnight. She might invite some boys to come by for a while, too. Her friend Tanya hesitated. Lauren told Tanya. "Just tell your mom you're spending the night at my house."

Tanya has to make a decision. It is a moral decision because it involves honesty. What are some of the influences that might affect her decision? Write your ideas here.

The first step in moral decision making is to *check out the influences* before making a choice. *Choice* is the key word here because by our very nature we are free to decide. As with every freedom we exercise, of course, there comes responsibility. As Catholics our first responsibility is to listen to Jesus and the Church, and to listen to our conscience.

Have the Facts

We should never be asked to make an important decision quickly. We need time to get information, gather the facts, and educate ourselves.

What if a young person at a party takes a drink, saying, "One beer is not going to affect my driving. I can handle it." What would be missing in this decision?

The young person does not know the facts. Depending on the circumstances, one beer can certainly affect the ability to drive safely.

The second step of moral decision making, then, is to educate oneself, to have the facts. So here are the first two things we should do:

Check out the influences.

Have the facts.

Others Can Help

Some people like to be fiercely independent when it comes to making decisions. "I can do it myself," they say. It's good to be independent, but we have to be wise, too. Wise people know when to ask for input, for advice. Nobody has all the answers.

Sometimes we can be poor judges when it comes to things that mean a great deal to us. This is called being *subjective*. This can be a problem when what is needed is the ability to step back and view the situation clearly, objectively. Someone else, especially someone with experience, is often better at doing that than we are. In the case of moral decisions, especially, it is wise to seek advice from a mature person we can trust.

Catholics are lucky because we can turn to the magisterium, the official teaching office of the Church. In a sometimes very stressful world whose values often stand in sharp contrast with the values of Jesus, we have the Church to instruct us, advise us, and give us moral support.

The third step of the decision-making process is to ask the advice of others.

Of course the trusted one who can help us better than anyone else is God. That is why an essential step in decision making for us as Catholics is asking God's help in prayer. You might be thinking, "But God doesn't answer my prayers." The truth is that God always answers our prayers. The answers, however, may not be the ones we want to hear.

The fourth step in decision making, then, is asking God's help in prayer. When we have an important decision to make, doesn't it make sense to bring it to the one who loves and cares for us beyond all others? Spend time in prayer before you make your choice. Ask yourself: What would Jesus do in this situation? Keep your prayer simple and focused. Then, above all, be quiet and listen.

Steps in moral decision making include:

Check out the influences.

Have the facts.

Others can help; seek advice.

In prayer ask God for help.

The Solitude of Christ, Maurice Denis, 1918

The Time Has Come

Now the time has come to *choose*, to make the decision. That is the fifth step of the process. If someone has sincerely tried to follow the first four steps, the choice should be clearer—not easier necessarily, but clearer.

One way to go about making the choice, especially in a truly important matter, is to make a list of all the pros and cons of a situation. Given all that you have learned in steps 1 to 4, that should be relatively simple to do. Here is an example:

Decision : To Smoke or Not to

Pros:	Cons:
I will smoke	**I will not smoke**
It's cool.	It's dumb.
My friends do it.	It's unhealthy.
I'm old enough.	It's expensive.
_____	_____
_____	_____

Now imagine you are the person making this decision about smoking. Using your list of pros and cons, make the decision. Use the knowledge, common sense, values, and faith you have, and make the best choice you can. Then act on your decision. Choice without action is not really a choice at all. When we choose, however, we must be willing to accept the consequences of our choice, good or bad.

There is one final step. After we have made our decision and acted on it, we need to give ourselves a little time to see the effects of our choice. Then we *evaluate* the decision. We ask, for example:

- How is this really working out for me?
- Am I happier? more at peace? Or do I feel uncomfortable or guilty? Why?
- Is God pleased with my choice?

It is true that people sometimes make choices that are so serious they cannot be completely changed or reversed. For example:

- Someone chooses drugs and becomes addicted. Recovery from the addiction is possible, of course, but the time—and sometimes the brain cells—the person has lost through addiction cannot be retrieved.
- Someone marries for the wrong reasons. The relationship is strained and unhappy. There are children. All these lives are affected forever.
- Someone decides to be promiscuous. The result is AIDS. There is no going back. The outcome is inevitable.

In such sad situations, even though the choices made cannot be changed, the person who made the choice can change, relying on God's sustaining love. New moral decisions can be made built on the experience. And these decisions can be wiser, more human, and more prayerful.

If you feel that your choice was the best one for you to make as a moral person, rejoice and be grateful! If you are not comfortable with the effects of your decision, don't be afraid to do something about it.

The most perfect model and guide we can have is Jesus Christ. He chose to live our human life completely. He knew what it was to be human, with all its joys and griefs, choices and temptations. After all he was once just your age. He wasn't immune to peer pressure, parental decisions, the desire for independence, and dreams of the future. In everything, however, he always kept before him the will of the Father.

Now we have explored the six steps of decision making. Whenever we have a moral choice to make, this is a process that will help us.

Check out the influences.

Have the facts.

Others can help; seek advice.

In prayer ask God for help.

Choose.

Evaluate your choice.

What is a moral choice? What makes it different from other choices?

What are the most important moral questions we must ask ourselves?

My Thoughts…

Now that you have completed this course on morality and have learned and applied the steps in moral decision making, perhaps you could share your experience and ideas of the moral life with another youth group in the parish or with young people from other churches in an ecumenical setting.

YOU ARE MY WITNESSES

Scripture My Life

Life can seem complicated at times, and its choices and problems can be overwhelming. Psalm 23 has often been a source of inspiration and comfort for many. Perhaps you, too, will find it helpful.

The LORD is my shepherd;
  there is nothing I lack.
In green pastures you let me graze;
  to safe waters you lead me;
  you restore my strength.
You guide me along the right path
  for the sake of your name.
Psalm 23:1–3

Catholic Teachings

Making Moral Decisions

Complete this list

Check_____

Have_____

Others_____

In_____

C_____

Evaluate_____

117

Something Worth Living For

World Youth Day

Where Am I Going?

Do you ever think about your future? Not many of us know at a very early age exactly what we are going to do with our lives. Usually, by the time we have grown out of childhood, we've changed our minds a dozen times.

What about you? Do you see any more clearly what your life is meant to be?

The very fact that you are a baptized Christian gives you a wonderful purpose in life. You are to be a follower of Christ—you are to bring his presence into the world. Now that sounds great—and it is. But, you ask, how is that going to be carried out in my life?

We are not talking only about what job or occupation or career you will have. That is only a part of your purpose. The deep-down questions for which you must find the answers are: How can I best follow Christ? To what do I wish to commit my life? What is my vocation?

The Church recognizes four vocations in which we can live out our baptismal call: marriage, the single life, the priesthood, and the religious life. Here we are going to concentrate specifically on the priesthood and the religious life.

Personality Profile

The priesthood and religious life are vocations that call us to a great adventure—the adventure of serving others as Jesus did. Obviously someone who thinks seriously about these vocations must be willing to grow as a person of prayer and love for Jesus in the Church. However, other gifts and strengths are necessary, too.

Take a moment to look at your personality—your gifts and your strengths. Circle the adjective in each pair below that best describes you. (Don't worry if some of these adjectives don't describe you!)

friendly	shy	loyal	uncommitted
talkative	quiet	open	secretive
calm	tense	hopeful	depressed
generous	selfish	sensitive	thoughtless
hardworking	lazy	responsible	unreliable
sense of humor	humorless	trusting	suspicious

Look over the words you have circled. Those in each left column show the gifts you already have. Those in the right columns suggest areas in which you can grow and change.

The Priesthood

Think of a priest you know and like. What do you suppose his life is like? What does he do all day? Why do you think he felt called to this life? Have you ever asked him about these things? Before you do, read on.

The special work of a priest is to bring God's saving love into our lives in ways we most need. In a parish a priest carries on the work of Christ by preaching the gospel, celebrating the sacraments, and leading the community in prayer. The priest brings Christ to us at key moments of our lives.

When a child is born or an adult wishes to become a Catholic, the priest welcomes them into the community of faith through Baptism. When we harm others and ourselves through sin, the priest, in the sacrament of Reconciliation, brings us the mercy and forgiveness of Christ. When we are troubled with illness or are facing death, the priest brings us the healing and consolation of Christ in the sacrament of the Anointing of the Sick. At so many moments of our lives, the priest is there acting in the person of Christ to bring God's love to us.

An Undivided Heart

A priest consecrates himself totally to God and to the service of the gospel. That is why priests make a promise of celibacy—a promise not to marry.

Celibacy is a sign of a wholehearted and faithful love for Christ and the freedom found in living for others. Through celibacy a priest is not to turn away from others; he turns toward Christ and loves Christ by serving others.

There are challenges and joys in every vocation, and the priesthood is no exception. Being a priest is not easy—no great life is—but it is immensely rewarding and blessed. The special joy of the priesthood is to be able to bring Christ to so many people in so many different ways. To do that well demands great generosity, deep love, and a passionate desire to serve God in others.

Religious Life

From the very beginning of the Church, some men and women have dedicated themselves to following Christ more closely. In wanting to imitate Christ, each tried in his or her own way to live the gospel life to the fullest with others in community.

The life they live is commonly called *religious life*. Religious priests, sisters, and brothers live a life totally consecrated to God. They share this life with others in a community so that they may support one another and minister in the Church together with greater strength and vigor.

How do they live? As a sign of giving themselves completely to God, religious men and women profess the evangelical counsels of poverty, chastity, and obedience. The Church reminds us that all Christians are called by Christ to a gospel, or evangelical, life. Religious, however, consecrate themselves publicly to live their vows of poverty, chastity, and obedience in the service of God's kingdom and as an example and reminder to all the world.

- By the vow of *poverty,* a religious freely promises to follow Christ, who lived simply and without wealth or status. Individual religious are not to own property and must have a deep respect for the proper use of this world's goods.
- By the vow of *chastity,* a religious freely chooses a life of loving service to the Church and his or her religious family. Chastity also includes a promise not to marry. In this way a religious should be free to share love with more people.
- By the vow of *obedience,* a religious freely chooses to listen carefully to God's direction in his or her life. By obedience to religious superiors and the Church, a religious man or woman is ready to serve anywhere in joy and love.

The Active Life

There are a variety of religious communities of men and women, each distinguished by some special mission, or apostolate, through which they serve the Church. There are religious communities that work with the poor, communities that serve the sick, communities whose ministry is preaching and giving retreats, and communities whose special mission is teaching.

Many religious communities also send their members all over the world to preach the gospel and serve the needs of people who may never have heard of Christ. The ministry of these communities is missionary work. For those who are ready and able, the religious life is an exciting way to follow Christ.

121

Contemplative Life

One of the oldest religious vocations in the Church is that of the *contemplative* life. What does it mean to be a contemplative religious?

In the early centuries of the Church, some Christians left their homes and possessions to live alone with God. They built hermitages and, later, monasteries in the solitude and peace of the desert. These people were the first contemplative religious. They lived apart from society and spent their time contemplating God in prayer, meditation, labor, and worship.

The vocation to the contemplative religious life is much the same today. Contemplative religious follow a life characterized by silence, manual labor, and above all, prayer. Contact with the outside world is limited in physical terms. In spiritual ways, however, contemplatives are intimately connected to the lives of others. They are very aware of all the sufferings, hopes, and concerns of the world, and they bring these to God in prayer each day.

It is a beautiful and challenging life. The contemplative vocation is a call to love and serve God and others in obscurity and prayer and silence. Contemplative religious are the great guardians of the Church. They support us all spiritually; they ask for nothing in return.

Prayer for Vocations

Theme: Something worth living for.

(All gather in a circle. Choose readers for each of the speakers. The readers form a circle within the circle. After each one speaks, he or she moves back into the larger circle.)

Song: "Be Not Afraid"

Leader: This prayer is based on a letter Sister Ita Ford, a Maryknoll missionary, wrote to her niece not too long before her death in El Salvador.

All: O God, help me to find that which
gives life a deep meaning for me.
Something worth living for; maybe
even worthy of dying for.
Something which energizes me,
exhausts me,
enables me to keep moving ahead.
I don't know what it might be—
that is for you to reveal to me, and for
me to find, to choose, to love.
Help me to begin looking and support
me in my search.

Speaker 1: **Mary, Mother of God**, you accepted God's invitation. You trusted, you believed, you were not afraid.

Response: O God, help me to find that which gives my life meaning, something worth living for.

Speaker 2: **Father Damien of Molokai**, you brought love, compassion, and hope to the lepers of Molokai. You gave your life for them. You trusted, you believed, you were not afraid. *(Response)*

Speaker 3: **Sisters Ita Ford**, **Maura Clarke**, **Dorothy Kazel**, and your companion, **Jean Donovan**, you risked your lives to help the poor in El Salvador. You were martyred there. You trusted, you believed, you were not afraid. *(Response)*

Speaker 4: **Saint Martin de Porres**, Dominican brother, you spent your life working with the poor, the sick, and the homeless. You are the saint of social justice. You trusted, you believed, you were not afraid. *(Response)*

Leader: There are many other priests, brothers, and sisters today who have found deep meaning in life—something worth living for. Take a few moments to think of someone you know whose life reveals what it means to live a vocation to the priesthood or religious life. Ask God to bless and strengthen them in trust, in faith, and in courage.

Song: Sing again the refrain from "Be Not Afraid."

GLORY to the FATHER, AND TO the SON, AND TO THE HOLY SPIRIT:

as it was in the beginning, is now,
and will be for ever.
Amen.

GLORY TO THE FATHER

COME, HOLY SPIRIT, FILL THE HEARTS OF YOUR FAITHFUL.

And kindle in them the fire of your love.

Send forth your Spirit and they shall be created.
And you will renew the face of the earth.

Let us pray.

Lord,
by the light of the Holy Spirit
you have taught the hearts of your faithful.
In the same Spirit
help us to relish what is right
and always rejoice in your consolation.

We ask this through Christ our Lord.
Amen.

COME HOLY SPIRIT

HAIL, MARY, FULL OF GRACE, THE LORD IS WITH YOU!

Blessed are you among women,
and blessed is the fruit of your womb, Jesus.
Holy Mary, mother of God,
pray for us sinners,
now and at the hour of our death.
Amen.

HAIL, MARY

I BELIEVE IN GOD, THE FATHER ALMIGHTY,

creator of heaven and earth.
I believe in Jesus Christ, his only Son,
our Lord.
He was conceived by the power of the
Holy Spirit
and born of the Virgin Mary.
He suffered under Pontius Pilate,
was crucified, died, and was buried.
He descended to the dead.
On the third day he rose again.
He ascended into heaven,
and is seated at the right hand of the Father.
He will come again to judge the living and
the dead.
I believe in the Holy Spirit,
the holy catholic Church,
the communion of saints,
the forgiveness of sins,
the resurrection of the body,
and the life everlasting.
Amen.

APOSTLES' CREED

OUR FATHER, WHO ART in HEAVEN, HALLOWED BE THY NAME;

thy kingdom come;
thy will be done on earth as it is in heaven.
Give us this day our daily bread;
and forgive us our trespasses
as we forgive those who trespass against us;
and lead us not into temptation,
but deliver us from evil.
Amen.

OUR FATHER

Hail, Holy Queen, Mother of Mercy,

hail, our life, our sweetness, and our hope.
To you we cry, the children of Eve:
to you we send up our sighs,
mourning and weeping in this land of exile.
turn, then, most gracious advocate,
your eyes of mercy toward us;
lead us home at last
and show us the blessed fruit of your
womb, Jesus:
O clement, O loving, O sweet Virgin Mary.

HAIL, HOLY QUEEN

The Angel Spoke God's Message to Mary,

and she conceived of the Holy Spirit.
Hail, Mary....

"I am the lowly servant of the Lord:
let it be done to me according to your word."
Hail, Mary....

And the Word became flesh
and lived among us.
Hail, Mary....

Pray for us, holy Mother of God,
that we may become worthy of the promises
of Christ.

Let us pray.

Lord,
fill our hearts with your grace:
once, through the message of an angel
you revealed to us the incarnation of your Son;
now, through his suffering and death
lead us to the glory of his resurrection.
We ask this through Christ our Lord.
Amen.

THE ANGELUS

My God, I Am Sorry for my Sins With All My Heart.

In choosing to do wrong
and failing to do good,
I have sinned against you
whom I should love above all things.
I firmly intend, with your help,
to do penance,
to sin no more,
and to avoid whatever leads me to sin.
Our Savior Jesus Christ
suffered and died for us.
In his name, my God, have mercy.

ACT OF CONTRITION

Lord, Make Me An Instrument of Your Peace:

where there is hatred, let me sow love;
where there is injury, pardon;
where there is doubt, faith;
where there is despair, hope;
where there is darkness, light;
where there is sadness, joy.
O divine Master, grant that I may not
so much seek
to be consoled as to console,
to be understood as to understand,
to be loved as to love.
For it is in giving that we receive,
it is in pardoning that we are pardoned,
it is in dying that we are born to eternal life.
Amen.

PRAYER OF SAINT FRANCIS

THE TEN COMMANDMENTS

1. I am the LORD your God: you shall not have strange Gods before me.

2. You shall not take the name of the LORD your God in vain.

3. Remember to keep holy the LORD's Day.

4. Honor your father and your mother.

5. You shall not kill.

6. You shall not commit adultery.

7. You shall not steal.

8. You shall not bear false witness against your neighbor.

9. You shall not covet your neighbor's wife.

10. You shall not covet your neighbor's goods.

Catechism of the Catholic Church

THE BEATITUDES

Blessed are the poor in spirit,
    for theirs is the kingdom of heaven.

Blessed are they who mourn,
    for they will be comforted.

Blessed are the meek,
    for they will inherit the land.

Blessed are they who hunger and thirst
        for righteousness,
    for they will be satisfied.

Blessed are the merciful,
    for they will be shown mercy.

Blessed are the clean of heart,
    for they will see God.

Blessed are the peacemakers,
    for they will be called children of God.

Blessed are they who are persecuted for the sake
        of righteousness,
    for theirs is the kingdom of heaven.

Matthew 5: 3–10

Index